CW01649580

FODOR'S®

COLORADO 1984

Fodor's Colorado:

Area Editor: CURTIS W. CASEWIT.
Editorial Contributors: JUNE JULIAN, BILL HOSOKAWA, TOM SZENTGYORGYI.
Editor: DEBRA BERNARDI.
Editorial Associate: MARY BETH BREWER.
Drawings: DAVID CANRIGHT, SANDRA LANG.
Maps and City Plans: DYNO LOWENSTEIN.

FODOR'S TRAVEL GUIDES
New York

Copyright © 1983 by FODOR'S TRAVEL GUIDES
ISBN 0-679-00997-3
ISBN 0-340-34124-6 (Hodder & Stoughton edition)
No part of this book may be reproduced in any form without permission in writing from the publisher.

All the following Guides are current (most of them also in the Hodder and Stoughton British edition.)

CURRENT FODOR'S COUNTRY AND AREA TITLES:

AUSTRALIA, NEW ZEALAND AND SOUTH PACIFIC
AUSTRIA
BELGIUM AND LUXEMBOURG
BERMUDA
BRAZIL
CANADA
CARIBBEAN AND BAHAMAS
CENTRAL AMERICA
EASTERN EUROPE
EGYPT
EUROPE
FRANCE
GERMANY
GREAT BRITAIN
GREECE
HOLLAND
INDIA
IRELAND
ISRAEL
ITALY
JAPAN
JORDAN AND HOLY LAND
KOREA
MEXICO
NORTH AFRICA
PEOPLE'S REPUBLIC OF CHINA
PORTUGAL
SCANDINAVIA
SCOTLAND
SOUTH AMERICA
SOUTHEAST ASIA
SOVIET UNION
SPAIN
SWITZERLAND
TURKEY
YUGOSLAVIA

CITY GUIDES:

BEIJING, GUANGZHOU, SHANGHAI
CHICAGO
DALLAS AND FORT WORTH
HOUSTON
LONDON
LOS ANGELES
MADRID
MEXICO CITY AND ACAPULCO
NEW ORLEANS
NEW YORK CITY
PARIS
ROME
SAN DIEGO
SAN FRANCISCO
STOCKHOLM, COPENHAGEN, OSLO, HELSINKI, AND REYKJAVIK
TOKYO
WASHINGTON, D.C.

FODOR'S BUDGET SERIES:

BUDGET BRITAIN
BUDGET CANADA
BUDGET CARIBBEAN
BUDGET EUROPE
BUDGET FRANCE
BUDGET GERMANY
BUDGET HAWAII
BUDGET ITALY
BUDGET JAPAN
BUDGET MEXICO
BUDGET SCANDINAVIA
BUDGET SPAIN
BUDGET TRAVEL IN AMERICA

USA GUIDES:

ALASKA
CALIFORNIA
CAPE COD
COLORADO
FAR WEST
FLORIDA
HAWAII
NEW ENGLAND
PENNSYLVANIA
SOUTH
TEXAS
USA (in one volume)

MANUFACTURED IN THE UNITED STATES OF AMERICA
10 9 8 7 6 5 4 3 2 1

CONTENTS

National Travel Club

Over 75 Years of Service To Our members

You Are Cordially Invited To Join!

Membership brings you 14 money-saving benefits and services INCLUDING a subscription to TRAVEL-HOLIDAY magazine AND $35,000 travel accident insurance coverage ($50,000 IMMEDIATELY with an initial 2-year membership) for ALL your travels ANYWHERE in the world and for the ENTIRE TERM of your membership. You enroll JUST ONCE (at incredibly low annual dues)—No monthly payments to make or bother about.

NO OTHER TRAVEL CLUB GIVES YOU SO MUCH FOR SO LITTLE

Over a HALF MILLION members consider these benefits indispensable:

- $35,000 Travel Accident Insurance ($50,000 on renewal; Immediately with initial 2-year membership
- Subscription to TRAVEL-HOLIDAY magazine
- Travel Information Service
- Book Discounts (25% savings)
- Routing Service
- Travel Digest Evaluation Program
- Avis & National Car Rental Discounts
- Mediguide Service
- Discount travel film Library
- Mail Forwarding Service
- Discount Pharmaceutical Service
- Discount Film Processing
- Car/Puter-Discount Auto Pricing & Buying Service
- Membership Card & Club Emblems

Accident insurance provided by Nationwide Insurance Company, Columbus, Ohio.

National Travel Club

Travel Building, Floral Park, N.Y. 11001

Please enroll me as a member for the term indicated:

☐ 1 Year **($35,000** travel accident insurance) $12.00
☐ 2 Years **($50,000** travel accident insurance) $23.00
☐ **I enclose remittance**

Charge to my ☐ Mastercard ☐ Visa ☐ Diner's ☐ American Express

Acct. # ____________________ Exp. Date ____________

Name ______________________________
(Signature if charging)

Address ______________________________

City ______________ State ________ Zip ________

FG-1A

Maupintour

Quality tours at home and abroad.

ESCORTED TOURS are fun. You enjoy yourself when you tour with a Maupintour group... and you have a choice of over 100 escorted holidays.

BETTER HOTELS, resorts, fine dining, special events, entertainment, luggage handling, tips, transfers... these are included with Maupintour.

NEW MAUPINTOUR BROCHURES. Be sure to read through the Maupintour brochures before you decide. Just write or phone for a copy. Then ask your Travel Agent for reservations on the Maupintour of your choice.

- ☐ Africa
- ☐ Alaska/Yukon
- ☐ Alps
- ☐ Arizona
- ☐ Australia
- ☐ Bavaria/Austria
- ☐ Belgium
- ☐ British Isles
- ☐ California
- ☐ Canada
- ☐ China
- ☐ Christmas Tours
- ☐ Colorado
- ☐ Cruise Tours
- ☐ Egypt/The Nile
- ☐ Europe
- ☐ Fall Foliage
- ☐ France
- ☐ Germany
- ☐ Greece/Aegean
- ☐ Hawaii
- ☐ Historic East
- ☐ Holland
- ☐ Iceland
- ☐ India/Nepal Kashmir
- ☐ Israel
- ☐ Italy
- ☐ Japan
- ☐ Middle East
- ☐ Morocco
- ☐ National Parks
- ☐ New Zealand
- ☐ Nile Cruise
- ☐ Opera Tours
- ☐ Orient
- ☐ Pacific N.W.
- ☐ Scandinavia
- ☐ South Pacific
- ☐ Spain/Portugal
- ☐ Switzerland
- ☐ USA East
- ☐ USA South
- ☐ USA West

Maupintour

quality escorted tours since 1951

Maupintour, P.O. Box 807, Lawrence, Ks. 66044. Telephone 800-255-4266.

FACTS AT YOUR FINGERTIPS

WHEN TO GO. Generally speaking, there is plenty of sunshine, and the humidity is low. This latter condition tends to cut down on discomfort in all but the highest temperature periods. Temperatures in the desert area of Colorado sometimes soar to the 100–115 mark, while some nearby mountain summits wear their stoles of ermine-white snow year round.

From Thanksgiving to the middle of April there is some of the best skiing in the country at some thirty Colorado areas and resorts.

Generally, average temperatures in winter are in the low 20's. Summer finds maximum temperatures in the mid-80's in the north to near 100 degrees in the south (in June, July, and August), with maximums in the 90's in surrounding months. But even in summer nights are cool, especially in the higher elevations.

PLANNING YOUR TRIP. If you don't want to bother with reservations on your own, a travel agent won't cost you a cent, except for specific charges like telegrams. The agent gets his fee from the hotel or carrier he books for you. A travel agent can also be of help for those who prefer to take their vacations on a "package tour"—thus keeping your own planning to a minimum. If you prefer the convenience of standardized accommodations, remember that the various hotel and motel chains publish free directories of their members that enable you to plan and reserve everything ahead of time.

If you don't belong to an auto club, now may be the time to join one. They can be very helpful about routings and providing emergency service on the road. In addition to its information services, the *American Automobile Association,* 8111 Gatehouse Rd., Falls Church, Va. 20042, has a nationwide network of some 26,000 service stations which provide emergency repair service.

The *Exxon Travel Club,* 4550 Decoma Ave., Houston, Texas 77002, provides information, low-cost insurance, and some legal services; and the *National Travel Club,* Travel Bldg., 51 Atlantic Ave., Floral Park, N.Y. 11001, offers information, insurance and tours.

The three major publishers of road atlases for the U.S. are Rand McNally, Hammond, and Grosset & Dunlap. Some of the major oil companies will send maps and mark preferred routes on them if you tell them what you have in mind. Try: *Exxon Touring Service,* 1251 Avenue of the Americas, New York, N.Y. 10020, or 4550 Decoma Ave., Houston, Texas 77001; *ARCO Travel Service,* P.O. Box 93, Versailles, Ky. 40383; *Texaco Travel Service,* P.O. Box 1459, Houston, Texas 77001; or *Mobil Oil Corp. Travel Service,* P.O. Box 25, Versailles, Ky. 40383. In addition, most states have their own maps, which pinpoint attractions, list historical sites, parks, etc. City chambers of commerce are also good sources of information. Specific addresses are given under *Tourist Information* in the individual state chapters.

Plan to board your pets, discontinue paper and milk deliveries, and tell your local police and fire departments when you'll be leaving and when you expect to return. Ask a kindly neighbor to keep an eye on your house or apartment; fully protect your swimming pool against intruders. Have a neighbor keep your mail, or have it held at the post office. Consider having your telephone temporarily disconnected if you plan to be away more than a few weeks. Look into the purchase of trip insurance (including baggage), and make certain your auto, fire, and other insurance policies are up to date. The AAA offers both personal accident insurance and bail bond protection as part of its annual membership. Today most people who travel use credit cards for important expenses such as gas, repairs, lodgings and some meals. Consider converting the greater portion of your trip money into travelers' checks. Arrange to have your lawn mowed at the usual times, and leave that kindly neighbor your itinerary (insofar as possible), car license number, and a key to your home (and tell police and firemen he has it). Since some hotel and motel chains give discounts (10%–25%) to Senior Citizens, be sure to have some sort of identification along if you qualify. Usually NARP or NRTA membership is best. (See below at the end of the hotels and motels section.)

PACKING. *What to take, what to wear.* Make a packing list for each member of the family. Then check off items as you pack them. It will save time, reduce confusion. Time-savers to carry along include extra photo film (plenty), suntan lotion, insect repellent, sufficient toothpaste, soap. Always carry an extra pair of glasses, including sunglasses, particularly if they're prescription ones. A travel iron is always a good tote-along, as are some transparent plastic bags (small and large) for wet suits, socks, etc. They are also excellent for packing shoes, cosmetics, and other easily damaged items. Fun extras to carry include binoculars, a compass, and a magnifying glass—useful in reading fine-print maps.

All members of the family should have sturdy shoes with nonslip soles. Keep them handy in the back of the car. Carry rain gear in a separate bag in the back of the car (so no one will have to get out and hunt for it in a downpour en route).

Women will probably want to stick to one or two basic colors for their wardrobes, so that they can manage with one set of accessories. If possible, include one knit or jersey dress or a pants suit. For dress-up evenings, take along a couple of "basic" dresses you can vary with a simple change of accessories. That way you can dress up or down to suit the occasion.

Be sure to check what temperatures will be like along the route. Traveling in mountains can mean cool evenings, even in summer—and so can traveling through the desert. An extra sweater is always a safe thing to pack, even if just to protect you from the air conditioning.

Men will probably want a jacket along for dining out, and a dress shirt and tie for formal occasions. Turtlenecks are now accepted almost everywhere and are a comfortable accessory. Don't forget extra slacks.

Planning a lot of sun time? Don't forget something to wear en route to the pool, beach, or lakefront, and for those first few days when you're getting reacquainted with Colorado's ultraviolet rays on tender skin.

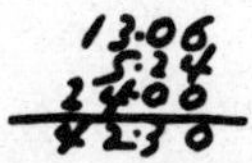

WHAT WILL IT COST? This is obviously a crucial question and one of the most difficult. A couple can travel comfortably in this section of the U.S. for about $80 a day (not counting gasoline or other transportation costs), as you can see in the table below.

In some areas you can cut expenses by traveling off season, when hotel rates are usually lower. The budget-minded traveler can also find bargain accommodations at tourist homes or family-style YMCA's and YWCA's. Some state and federal parks also provide inexpensive lodging. And in this 7-state area 11 colleges offer dormitory accommodations to tourists during the summer vacations at single-room rates of $5–$15 per night with meals from $1 to $5.00. A directory of some 200 such bargains all over the U.S. is *Mort's Guide to Low-Cost*

Vacations and Lodgings on College Campuses, USA-Canada, from Mort Barish Associates, Inc., Research Park, State Rd., Princeton, N.J. 08540.

Another way to cut down on the cost of your trip is to look for out-of-the-way resorts. Travelers are frequently rewarded by discovering very attractive areas which haven't as yet begun to draw quantities of people.

Typical Expenses for Two People

Room at *moderate* hotel or motel	$34.00
Breakfast, including tip	4.00
Lunch at *inexpensive* restaurant, including tip	9.00
Dinner at *moderate* restaurant, including tip	18.00
Sightseeing bus tour	14.00
An evening drink	3.00
Admission to museum or historic site	5.00
	$87.00

If you are budgeting your trip, don't forget to set aside a realistic amount for the possible rental of sports equipment (perhaps including a boat or canoe), entrance fees to amusement and historical sites, etc. Allow for tolls for bridges and superhighways (this can be a major item), extra film for cameras, and souvenirs.

After lodging, your next biggest expense will be food, and here you can make very substantial economies if you are willing to get along with only one meal a day (or less) in a restaurant. Plan to eat simply, and to picnic. It will save you time and money, and it will help you enjoy your trip more. That beautiful scenery does not have to whiz by at 55 miles per hour. Many states have picnic and rest areas, often well-equipped and in scenic spots, even on highways and thruways, so finding a pleasant place to stop is usually not difficult. Before you leave home put together a picnic kit.

Sturdy plastic plates and cups are cheaper in the long run than throw-away paper ones; and the same goes for permanent metal flatware rather than the throw-away plastic kind. Pack a small electric pot and two thermoses, one for water and one for milk, tea, or coffee. In other words, one hot, and one cold. If you go by car, take along a small cooler. Bread, milk, cold cereal, jam, tea or instant coffee, fruit, fresh vegetables that need no cooking (such as lettuce, cucumbers, carrots, tomatoes, and mushrooms), cold cuts, cheese, nuts, raisins, eggs (hard boil them in the electric pot in your room the night before)—with only things like these you can eat conveniently, cheaply, and well.

Sooner or later, however, you will wind up eating in a restaurant, and even there there are a number of things you can do to cut costs. 1) Order a complete dinner; a la carte *always* adds up to more. If the place doesn't have complete dinners, don't eat there. 2) If there is a salad bar, you can fill up there and save the price of dessert and/or extras. 3) Ask about smaller portions, at reduced prices, for children. More and more places are providing them now. 4) Go to a Chinese restaurant and order *one less* main dish than the number of people in your group. You'll still come away pleasantly full. 5) Always stop at the cash register and look over the menu *before* you sit down. 6) Ask for the Day's Special, the House Special, Chef's Special or whatever it's called. Chances are that it will be better and more abundant than the other things on the menu. 7) Have a few standard items like coffee, fruit juice, ice cream, to test the price range. 8) Remember that in better restaurants lunch may be more of a bargain than dinner. 9) Below, in the section on restaurants, we suggest some chains that offer good value for your money.

If you like a drink before dinner or bed, bring your own bottle. Most hotels and motels supply ice free or for very little, but the markup on alcoholic beverages in restaurants, bars, lounges and dining rooms is enormous, and in some states peculiar laws apply regarding alcohol consumption. And in any case, a good domestic dry white wine makes a fine aperitif and can be far cheaper than a cocktail.

HINTS TO THE MOTORIST. Probably the first precaution you will take is to have your car thoroughly checked by your regular dealer or service station to make sure that everything is in good shape. Second, you may find it wise to join an auto club that can provide you with trip planning information, insurance coverage, and emergency and repair service along the way. If you are a member of the NRTA/AARP, that organization has a motoring plan in cooperation with the Amoco Motor Club that offers a number of emergency and repair services. Write to NRTA/AARP, P.O. Box 28264, Raleigh, N.C. 27611, or call 1–800–334–3300.

You may encounter signs reading, "Four-wheel drive vehicles only beyond this point." This is wild, rugged country, where you follow routes, not roads, through shifting sand, up trickling stream beds which can turn into raging torrents during a sudden storm, where the wheels of even four-wheel drive vehicles can sink hopelessly into the sand if they don't move along briskly, and where you may have to climb a 27-degree face of sheer rock. This is an area where, off the well-traveled, well-kept main roads, the motorist can have virtually any driving experience he cares to meet.

DESERT DRIVING

You will encounter long stretches of desert driving in the southern portions of Colorado. Better cars, better roads, and more service facilities make desert driving less a hazard than it once was. A principal point to check before crossing the hot desert is your tires. Put them at normal driving pressure or slightly below. Heat builds pressure. If your car seems to be bouncing too readily, stop to let your tires cool. If you have a good radiator, don't worry about extra water, but keep an eye on the water gauge. Be alert for sudden sandstorms and rainstorms. If you have a car radio, keep it tuned to local stations for information about unusual road conditions. In spite of its dryness, the desert, in a flash flood, can become a death trap. In sandstorms, pull off the road and wait it out.

MOUNTAIN DRIVING

Unless you venture onto more rugged mountain roads, you should have little trouble with mountain driving. Today's mountain highways are engineered for the ordinary driver. They are normally wide, well graded, and safe. Be especially wary of exceeding the speed limits posted for curves. Keep to the right. If your normal driving is at low altitudes, have a garage mechanic check your carburetor. It may need adjusting for mountain driving. Use your motor for downhill runs, second or low gear to save your brakes. If your car stalls, and your temperature gauge is high, it could mean a vapor lock. Cover the fuel pump with a damp cloth for a few minutes.

If you get stuck on any kind of road, pull off the highway onto the shoulder, raise the hood, attach something white (a handkerchief, scarf, or a piece of tissue) to the door handle on the driver's side, and sit inside and wait. This is especially effective on limited-access highways, usually patrolled vigilantly by state highway officers. A special warning to women stalled at night: Remain inside with the doors locked, and make sure the Good Samaritan is indeed what he seems. It is easier to find telephones along the major highways these days, since their locations are more frequently marked than they used to be. If you're a member of an automobile club, call the nearest garage listed in your emergency directory. Or ask the operator for help.

PULLING A TRAILER

If you plan to pull a trailer (boat or house) on your holiday trip, and have never done so before, don't just hook up and set out. You need a whole new set of driving skills—starting, stopping, cornering, passing, *being* passed, and, most tricky of all, backing. Reading about it will help a little, but not much. Try to practice in an open field or empty parking lot, but if this is not possible, take your maiden trip in light traffic. A few useful hints: In starting and stopping, do everything a little more slowly and gradually than is normal; in cornering, swing wider than usual, remembering the trailer won't follow exactly the rear wheels of the towing car. Too sharp a right turn will put your trailer wheels on the curb. In passing, remember you're longer than usual. Allow more safe distance ahead to pull back into the right lane. A slight bit of extra steering will help if you're *being* passed by a large truck or bus. In this situation, the trailer is inclined to sway from air currents. Don't worsen it by slowing down. It's better to speed up slightly. In backing, the basic technique is to turn the steering wheel opposite to the way you would want the car to go if you were driving it alone. From there on, it's practice, practice, practice. Most states have special safety regulations for trailers, and these change frequently. If you plan to operate your trailer in several states, check with your motor club, the police, or the state motor vehicle department about the rules. Also talk it over with the dealer from whom you buy or lease your trailer. Generally, speed limits for cars hauling trailers are lower, parking of trailers (and automobiles) is prohibited on expressways, and tunnels bar trailers equipped with cooking units which use propane gas.

PETS AND PACKING

Traveling by car with your pet dog or cat? More and more motels accept them but be sure to check before you register. Some turn them down, some want to look first, some offer special facilities. If it's a first-time trip for your pet, accustom it to car travel by short trips in your neighborhood. And when you're packing, include its favorite food, bowls, and toys. Discourage your dog from riding with its head out the window. Wind and dust particles can permanently damage its eyes. Don't leave your pet in a parked car on a hot day while you dawdle over lunch. Keep his bowl handy for water during stops for gas; gasoline attendants are usually very cooperative about this. Make sure your pet exercises periodically; this is a good way for you and the kids to unwind from long stretches of unbroken traveling, too.

One tip for frequent motel stops along the road is to pack two suitcases—one for the final destination, and the other with items for overnight stops: pajamas, shaving gear, cosmetics, toothbrushes, fresh shirt or dress. Put the overnight luggage into the trunk last, so it can be pulled out first on overnight stops. A safety hint: Don't string your suits and dresses on hangers along a chain or rod stretched across the back seat. This obstructs vision and can cause accidents.

HOTELS AND MOTELS. General Hints. It's better not to take potluck for lodgings. You'll waste a lot of time hunting for a place, and often won't be happy with the accommodations you finally find. If you are without reservations, by all means begin looking early in the afternoon. If you have reservations, but expect to arrive later than five or six P.M., advise the hotel or motel in advance. Some places will not, unless advised, hold reservations after six P.M. And if you hope to get a room at the hotel's *minimum* rate be sure to reserve ahead or arrive very early.

If you are planning to stay in a popular resort region, at the height of the season, reserve well in advance. Include a deposit for all places except motels (and for motels if they request one). Many chain or associated motels and hotels will make advance reservations for you at affiliated hostelries along your route.

A number of hotels and motels have one-day laundry and dry-cleaning services, and many motels have coin laundries. Most motels, but not all, have telephones in the rooms. If you want to be sure of room service, however, better stay at a hotel. Many motels have swimming pools, and even beachfront hotels frequently have a pool. Even some motels in the heart of large cities have pools. An advantage at motels is the free parking. There's seldom a charge for parking at country and resort hotels.

Hotel and motel chains. In addition to the hundreds of excellent independent motels and hotels throughout the country, there are also many that belong to national or regional chains. A major advantage of the chains, to many travelers, is the ease of making reservations en route, or at one fell swoop in advance. If you are a guest at a member hotel or motel, the management will be delighted to secure you a sure booking at one of its affiliated hotels for the coming evening at no cost to you. Chains also usually have toll-free WATS (800) lines to assist you in making reservations on your own. This, of course, saves you time, worry, and money. In some chains, you have the added advantage of knowing what the standards are all the way. The insistence on uniform standards of comfort, cleanliness, and amenities is more common in motel than in hotel chains. (Easy to understand when you realize that most hotel chains are formed by buying up older, established hotels, while most motel chains have control of their units from start to finish.) This is not meant to denigrate the hotel chains; after all, individuality can be one of the great charms of a hotel. Some travelers, however, prefer independent motels and hotels because they are more likely to reflect the character of the surrounding area.

Since the single biggest expense of your whole trip is lodging, you may well be discouraged and angry at the prices of some hotel and motel rooms, particularly when you know you are paying for things you neither need nor want, such as a heated swimming pool, wall-to-wall carpeting, a huge color TV set, two huge double beds for only two people, meeting rooms, a cocktail lounge, maybe even a putting green. Nationwide, motel prices for two people now average $37 a night; hotel prices run from $35 to $85, with the average around $52. This explains the recent rapid spread of a number of budget motel chains whose rates average $17.50 for a single, $21 for a double, an obvious advantage.

The main national motel chains are Holiday Inn, Howard Johnson's; Quality Courts, Ramada Inns, Sheraton Motor Inns, and TraveLodge. Alongside the style that these places represent, however, are others, less luxurious and less costly. Here are the ones which operate in this seven-state area: Budget Host Inns, Box 16656, Fort Worth, Texas 76114, call (817) 626-7064; Western 6 Motels, 1156 7th Ave., Hacienda Heights, California 91745, call (213) 961-1681; Days Inns of America, Inc., 2751 Buford Highway, Northeast, Atlanta 1, Georgia 30324, call 1-800-325-2525; E-Z 8 Motels, 2484 Hotel Circle Place, San Diego, California 92108, call (619) 291-8252; Friendship Inns International, 739 South Fourth, West, Salt Lake City, Utah 84101, call (800) 453-4511; Imperial 400 National, Inc., 1830 North Nash Street, Arlington, Virginia 22209, call (800) 368-4400; Interstate Inns, P.O. Box 760, Kimball, Nebraska 69145, call (308) 235-4616; LaQuinta Motor Inns, P.O. Box 32064, San Antonio, Texas 78216, call (800) 531-5900; Regal 8 Inns, P.O. Box 1268, Mount Vernon, Illinois 62864, call (618) 242-7240; Super 8 Motels, 1700 El Camino Real, Suite 503, San Diego, California 94902, call 1-800-843-1991; Magic Key Inns of America, 5 North First Ave., Yakima, Washington 98902, call (509) 248-7421.

Prices in the budget chains are fairly uniform, but this is not the case in chains such as Ramada, Quality, Holiday Inn, Howard Johnson and TraveLodge. Their prices vary widely by region, location and season. Among the national non-budget chains the most expensive are Hilton, Marriott and Sheraton; the middle range includes Holiday Inn, Howard Johnson, Quality Inn and TraveLodge; and the least expensive are usually Best Western, Ramada and Rodeway.

HOTEL AND MOTEL CATEGORIES

Hotels and motels in all the Fodor guidebooks to the U.S.A. are divided into five categories, arranged primarily by price, but also taking into consideration the degree of comfort, the amount of service, and the atmosphere which will surround you in the establishment of your choice. Occasionally, an establishment with *deluxe* prices will offer only *expensive* service or atmosphere, and so we will list it as *expensive.* On the other hand, a hotel which charges only *moderate* prices may offer superior comfort and service, so we will list it as *expensive.* Our ratings are flexible and subject to change. We should also point out that many fine hotels and motels have to be omitted for lack of space.

Although the names of the various hotel and motel categories are standard throughout this series, the prices listed under each category may vary from area to area. This variance is meant to reflect local price standards, and take into account that what might be considered a *moderate* price in a large urban area might be quite *expensive* in a rural region. In every case, however, the dollar ranges for each category are clearly stated before each listing of establishments.

Super Deluxe: This category is reserved for only a few hotels. In addition to giving the visitor all the amenities discussed under the deluxe category (below), the super deluxe hotel has a special atmosphere of glamor, good taste, and dignity. Its history will inevitably be full of many anecdotes, and it will probably be a favored meeting spot of local society. In short, super deluxe means the tops.

Deluxe. The minimum facilities must include bath and shower in all rooms, valet and laundry service, suites available, a well-appointed restaurant and a bar (where local law permits), room service, TV and telephone in room, air conditioning and heat (unless locale makes one or the other unnecessary), pleasing decor, and an atmosphere of luxury, calm, and elegance. There should be ample and personalized service. In a deluxe *motel,* there may be less service rendered by employees and more by automatic machines (such as refrigerators and icemaking machines in your room), but there should be a minimum of do-it-yourself in a truly deluxe establishment.

Expensive. All rooms must have bath or shower, valet and laundry service, restaurant and bar (local law permitting), limited room service, TV and telephone in room, heat and air conditioning (locale not precluding), pleasing decor. Although decor may be as good as that in deluxe establishments, hotels and motels in this category are frequently designed for commercial travelers or for families in a hurry and are somewhat impersonal in terms of service. As for *motels* in this category, valet and laundry service will probably be lacking; the units will be outstanding primarily for their convenient location and functional character, not for their attractive or comfortable qualities.

(*Note:* We often list top-notch ultra-modern hotels in this category, in spite of the fact that they have rates as high as deluxe hotels and motels. We do this because certain elements are missing in these hotels—usually service. In spite of automated devices such as ice-cube-making machines and message-signaling buzzers, service in these hotels is not up to the standard by which we judge deluxe establishments. Room service is incredibly slow in some of these places, and the entire atmosphere is often one of expediency over comfort, economy of manpower and overhead taking precedence over attention to the desires of guests.)

Moderate. Each room should have an attached bath or shower, there should be a restaurant *or* coffee shop, TV available, telephone in room, heat and air conditioning (locale not precluding), relatively convenient location, clean and comfortable rooms, and public rooms. *Motels* in this category may not have attached bath or shower, may not have a restaurant or coffee shop (though one is usually nearby), and, of course, may have no public rooms to speak of.

Inexpensive. Nearby bath or shower, telephone available, clean rooms are the minimum.

Free parking is assumed at all motels and motor hotels; you must pay for parking at most city hotels, though certain establishments have free parking, frequently for occupants of higher-than-minimum-rate rooms. *Baby sitter* lists are always available in good hotels and motels, and *cribs* for the children are always on hand—sometimes at no cost, but more frequently at a cost of $1 or $2 per night. The cost of a *cot* in your room, to supplement the beds, is around $3 per night, but moving an *extra single bed* into a room costs around $7 in better hotels and motels.

Senior citizens may in some cases receive special discounts on lodgings. The Days Inn chain offers various discounts to anyone 55 or older. Holiday Inns give a 10% discount year-round to members of the NRTA (write to National Retired Teachers Association, Membership Division, 701 North Montgomery St., Ojai, California 93023) and the AARP (write to American Association of Retired Persons, Membership Division, 215 Long Beach Blvd., Long Beach, California 90802). Members of the AARP, the NRTA, the National Association of Retired Persons, the Catholic Golden Age of United Societies of U.S.A., and the Old Age Security Pensioners of Canada and similar organizations benefit increasingly from a number of discounts, but the amounts, sources and availability of these change, so it is best to check with either your own organization or with the hotel, motel or restaurant chain you plan to use. The *National Council of Senior Citizens,* 1511 K St. N.W., Washington, D.C. 20025, works especially to develop low-cost travel possibilities for its members.

The closest thing America has to Europe's bed-and-breakfast is the private houses that go by the various names of tourist home, guest home, or guest house. These are often large, still fairly elegant old homes in quiet residential or semiresidential parts of larger towns or along secondary roads and the main streets of small towns and resorts. Styles and standards vary widely, of course; generally, private baths are less common and rates are pleasingly low. In many small towns such guest houses are excellent examples of the best a region has to offer of its own special atmosphere. Each one will be different, so that their advantage is precisely the opposite of that "no surprise" uniformity which motel chains pride themselves on. Few, if any, guests houses have heated pools, wall-to-wall carpeting, or exposed styrofoam-wooden beams in the bar. Few if any even have bars. What you do get, in addition to economy, is the personal flavor of a family atmosphere in a private home. In popular tourist areas, state or local tourist information offices or chambers of commerce usually have lists of homes that let out spare rooms to paying guests, and such a listing usually means that the places on it have been inspected and meet some reliable standard of cleanliness, comfort, and reasonable pricing. A helpful book is *Bed and Breakfast U.S.A.: A Guide to Guest Houses and Tourist Homes,* is available from Tourist House Associates of America, Inc., P.O. Box 335-A, Greentown, Pennsylvania 18426. These places are more common in the eastern U.S. than in the Rockies and Plains area, but you will find some in this region as well.

In larger towns and cities a good bet for clean, plain, reliable lodging is a YMCA or YWCA. These buildings are usually centrally located, and their rates tend to run to less than half of those of hotels. Nonmembers are welcome, but may pay slightly more than members. A few very large Ys may have accommodations for couples but usually sexes are segregated. Decor is spartan and the cafeteria fare plain and wholesome, but a definite advantage is the use of the building's pool, gym, reading room, information services, and other facilities. For a directory, write to National Council of the YMCA, 291 Broadway, New York, N.Y. 10007; and the National Board of the YWCA, 135 W. 50th St., New York, N.Y. 10020.

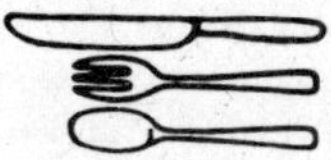

DINING OUT. For evening dining, the best advice is to make reservations whenever possible. Most hotels and farm-vacation places have set dining hours. For motel stayers, life is simpler if the motel has a restaurant. If it hasn't, try to stay at one that is near a restaurant.

Some restaurants are fussy about customers' dress, particularly in the evening. For women, pants and pants suits are now almost universally acceptable. For men, tie and jacket remains the standard, but turtleneck sweaters are becoming more and more common. Shorts are almost always frowned on for both men and women. Standards of dress are becoming more relaxed, so a neatly dressed customer will usually experience no problem. If in doubt about accepted dress at a particular establishment, call ahead.

Roadside stands, turnpike restaurants, and cafeterias have no fixed standards of dress.

If you're traveling with children, you may want to find out if a restaurant has a children's menu and commensurate prices (many do).

When figuring the tip on your check, base it on the total charges for the meal, not on the grand total, if that total includes a sales tax. Don't tip on tax.

RESTAURANT CATEGORIES

The restaurants mentioned in this volume which are located in large metropolitan areas are categorized by type of cuisine: French, Chinese, Armenian, etc., with restaurants of a general nature listed as American-International.

Restaurants in less populous areas are divided into price categories as follows: *super deluxe, deluxe, expensive, moderate,* and *inexpensive.* As a general rule, expect restaurants in metropolitan areas to be higher in price, but many restaurants that feature foreign cuisine are surprisingly inexpensive. We should also point out that limitations of space make it impossible to include every establishment. We have, therefore, listed those which we recommend as the best within each price range.

Although the names of the various restaurant categories are standard throughout this series, the prices listed under each category may vary from area to area. This variation is meant to reflect local price standards and take into account that what might be considered a *moderate* price in a large urban area might be quite *expensive* in a rural region. In every case, however, the dollar ranges for each category are clearly stated before each listing of establishments.

Super Deluxe. This category will probably be pertinent to only one or two metropolitan areas. It indicates an outstanding restaurant which is lavishly decorated, which may delight in the fear it inspires among the humble. Frequently over-priced and over-rated, it will charge the customer at least $12 for soup, entrée, and dessert. The average price for the same is apt to be closer to $16, although some will run much higher than this. As in all other categories, this price range does not include cocktails, wines, cover or table charges, tip, or extravagant house specialties. The price range here indicates a typical roast-beef (prime ribs) dinner. The restaurant in this category must have a superb wine list, excellent service, immaculate kitchens, and a large, well-trained staff.

Deluxe. Many a fine restaurant around the country falls into this category. It will have its own well-deserved reputation for excellence, perhaps a house specialty or two for which it is famous, and an atmosphere of elegance or unique decor. It will have a good wine list where the law permits, and will be considered the best in town by the inhabitants. It will have a clean kitchen and attentive staff.

Expensive. In addition to the expected dishes, it will offer one or two house specialties, wine list, and cocktails (where law permits), air conditioning (unless locale makes it unnecessary), a general reputation for very good food and an adequate staff, an elegant decor, and appropriately dressed clientele.

Moderate. Cocktails and/or beer where law permits, air conditioning (when needed), clean kitchen, adequate staff, better-than-average service. General reputation for good, wholesome food.

Inexpensive. The bargain place in town, it is clean, even if plain. It will have air conditioning (when necessary), tables (not a counter), and a clean kitchen and will attempt to provide adequate service.

Chains. There are now several chains of restaurants, some of them nationwide, which offer reliable eating at excellent budget prices. Look for them as you travel, and check local telephone directories in cities where you stop. Some of them are: 1) *Arthur Treacher's Fish and Chips* (limited menu, but very low prices, and expanding rapidly); 2) *Far West Services* (individual restaurants are usually named *Moonraker* or *Plankhouse;* lunch is a better bargain than dinner); 3) *Mr. Steak;* 4) *Sambo's* (simple food but surprisingly inexpensive); 5) *Sheraton* and *Holiday Inn* motels and hotels have all-you-can-eat, fixed-price buffets on certain days. Check locally.

LOCAL TIME. Colorado is on Mountain Time.

SUMMER SPORTS. Swimming is invigorating in many of the lakes and reservoirs and relaxing in the hot springs pools in Colorado. Water skiing and sailing are popular on the larger lakes. Sailing is available on the lakes created by the many dams and on some reservoirs as well.

The many rivers and streams offer exciting possibilities for **canoeing, kayaking,** and **rafting.**

The Rocky Mountains offer ample opportunity for **hiking, backpacking,** and **mountain climbing** or **horseback riding.** Many areas are accessible only on foot or by horse.

Fishing in this area is very popular and the system of waterways quite extensive; whether your pleasure is fly fishing the rivers and streams for trout or fishing the lakes for the larger walleye, bass, and northern pike, you're certain of great sport and much excitement.

In light of this area's western frontier heritage, it's not surprising that **rodeo** is the most pervasive of the spectator sports throughout this region. In general the season runs from late spring into early fall.

There are many fine **golf** courses throughout the area. **Tennis** is also a popular sport, and courts are found at virtually every major resort or urban area.

WINTER SPORTS. Skiing is without a doubt the major winter sport of this area. New areas continue to be developed throughout the Rocky Mountains, especially Aspen and Vail. Cross-country skiing, or **ski touring,** is becoming increasingly popular as both a means of escape from the cost of lift tickets and the ever-longer lift lines, and also as a means of enjoying the breathtaking scenery.

Each year, **snowmobiling** attracts more and more people who enjoy the thrill of speeding along snow-covered mountain trails or over open meadows. Many areas have organized rallies and races.

Ice skating on frozen lakes and ponds, or in year-round rinks, also has its share of enthusiasts.

Hunting for deer, antelope, elk, moose, and even bear brings hunters from all over into this area. There are also seasons for waterfowl, pheasant, quail, partridge, and grouse. In some cases, nonresidents are permitted to hunt the less populous of these species only with bow and arrows.

ROUGHING IT. More, and improved, camping facilities are springing up each year across the country, in national parks, national forests, state parks, in private camping areas, and trailer parks, which by now have become national institutions. Farm vacations continue to gain adherents, especially among families with children. Some accommodations are quite deluxe, some extremely simple. Here and there a farm has a swimming pool, while others have facilities for trailers and camping. For a directory of farms which take vacationers (including details of rates, accommodations, dates, etc.), write to *Adventure Guides, Inc.,* 36 East 57 Street, New York, N.Y. 10022 for their 224-page book *Farm Ranch & Country Vacations.*

Because of the great size of the United States and the distances involved, youth hostels have not developed in this country the way they have in Europe and Japan. In the entire 3½ million square miles of the U.S. there are upwards of 200 youth hostels and because they are, in any case, designed primarily for people who are traveling under their own power, usually hiking or bicycling, rather than by car or commercial transportation, they tend to be away from towns and cities and in rural areas, near scenic spots. Although their members are mainly younger people, there is no age limit. You must be a member to use youth hostels; write to *American Youth Hostel Association, Inc.,* 1332 I St., N.W., 8th Floor, Washington, D.C. 20005. A copy of the Hostel Guide and Handbook will be included in your membership. Accommodations are simple, dormitories are segregated by sex, common rooms and kitchen are shared, and everyone helps with the cleanup. Lights out 11 P.M. to 7 A.M., no alcohol or other drugs allowed. Membership fees: under 18–$7; 18 and over–$14; family–$21. Hostel rates vary; $3.50 is average. In season it is wise to reserve ahead; write or phone to the particular hostel you plan to stay in. Most of the hostels are in the piedmont belt.

Useful Addresses: *National Parks Service,* U.S. Dept. of the Interior, 18th and C St. N.W., Washington, D.C. 20240; *National Forest Service,* U.S. Dept. of Agriculture, Washington, D.C. 20250. For information on state parks, write *State Parks Dept., State Office Building* in the capital of the state in which you are interested.

The National Campers & Hikers Assoc., 7172 Transit Rd., Buffalo, N.Y. 14221. Commercial camping organizations include *American Camping Assoc., Inc.,* Bradford Woods, Martinsville, Indiana 46151, and *Kampgrounds of America, Inc.,* P.O. Box 30558, Billings, Montana 59114.

TIPPING. Tipping is supposed to be a personal thing, your way of expressing your appreciation of someone who has taken pleasure and pride in giving you attentive, efficient, and personal service. When you get genuinely good service, feel secure in rewarding it, and when you feel that the service you got was slovenly, indifferent, or surly, don't hesitate to show this by the size, or withholding, of your tip. Remember that in many places the help are paid very little and depend on tips for the better part of their income. This is supposed to give them incentive to serve you well. These days, the going rate for tipping on *restaurant* service is 15% on the amount *before* taxes. Tipping at counters is not universal, but many people leave $0.25 on anything up to $1, and 10% on anything over that. For *bellboys,* 50¢ per bag is usual. However, if you load him down with all manner of bags, hatboxes, cameras, coats, etc., you might consider giving an extra quarter or two. For one-night stays in most *hotels* and *motels,* you leave nothing. But if you stay longer, at the end of your stay leave the maid $1–$1.25 per day, or $7 per person per week for multiple occupancy. If you are staying at an *American Plan* hostelry (meals included), $1.50 per day per person for the waiter or waitress is considered sufficient, and is left at the end of your stay. If you have been surrounded by an army of servants (one bringing relishes, another rolls, etc.), add a few extra dollars and give the lump sum to the captain or *maître d'hôtel* when you leave, asking him to allocate it.

For the many other services you may encounter in a big hotel or resort, figure roughly as follows: doorman, 25¢ for taxi handling, 50¢ for help with baggage; bellhop, 50¢ per bag, more if you load him down with extras; parking attendant, 50¢; bartender, 15%; room service, 10–15% of that bill; laundry or valet service, 15%; pool attendant, 50¢ per day; snackbar waiter at pool, beach, or golf club, 50¢ per person for food and 15% of the beverage check; locker attendant, 50¢ per person per day, or $2.50 per week; masseur or masseuse 20% of the bill; golf caddies, $2–$3 per bag, or 15% of the greens fee for an 18-hole course, or $3 on a free course; barbers, 50¢; shoeshine attendants, 25¢; hairdressers, $1.50; manicurists, $1.

Transportation. Give 25¢ for any taxi fare under $1 and 15% for any above. Limousine service, 20%. Car rental agencies, nothing. Bus porters are tipped 25¢ per bag, drivers nothing. On charters and package tours, conductors and drivers usually get $5–$10 per day from the group as a whole, but be sure to ask whether this has already been figured into the package cost. On short local sightseeing runs, the driver-guide may get 50¢ per person, more if you think he has been especially helpful or personable. Airport bus drivers, nothing. Redcaps, 50¢. Tipping at curbside check-in is unofficial, but same as above. On the plane, no tipping.

Railroads suggest you leave 10–15% per meal for dining car waiters, but the steward who seats you is not tipped. Sleeping-car porters get about $1 per person per night. The 25¢ or 35¢ you pay a railway station baggage porter is not a tip but the set fee that he must hand in at the end of the day along with the ticket stubs he has used. Therefore his tip is anything you give him above that, 25–50¢ per bag, depending on how heavy your luggage is.

HINTS TO HANDICAPPED TRAVELERS. Important sources of information in this field are: 1) the books: *Travel Ability,* by Lois Reamy, published by Macmillan Publishing Co., Inc., 101K Brown St., Riverside, NJ 08370. and *Access to the World: A Travel Guide for the Handicapped,* by Louise Weiss, available from Facts on File, 460 Park Avenue South, New York, N.Y. 10016, $14.95. 2) the *Travel Information Center,* Moss Rehabilitation Hospital,

12th Street and Tabor Road, Philadelphia, Penn. 19141. 3) *Easter Seal Society for Crippled Children and Adults,* Director of Education and Information Service, 2023 West Ogden Avenue, Chicago, Illinois 60612.

In addition, another publication which gives valuable information about motels, hotels, and restaurants (rating them, telling about steps, table heights, door widths, etc.) is the annually revised guide *The Wheelchair Traveler,* by Douglass R. Annand, Ball Hill Road, Milford, N.H. 03055. Many of the nation's national parks have special facilities for the handicapped. These are described in *National Park Guide for the Handicapped,* available from the U.S. Government Printing Office, Washington, D.C. 20402.

PHOTOGRAPHY. In the high altitude and low humidity of Colorado, the air is clear and thin and there is an abundance of ultra-violet light which, though invisible, is picked up as a blue haze by colorfilm. The use of a skylight filter cuts out these rays, and your pictures will appear normal. The light at these high altitudes is very bright, and pictures of sunlit scenes require ½ to 1 full stop less exposure than you would ordinarily use. If you can afford the extra cost in film of exposing stop over and under in addition to what seems to be the correct exposure, you are nearly certain of getting a perfectly exposed photograph. Professional photographers often use this technique.

If your camera has interchangeable lenses, a wide-angle lens can capture not only the broad panoramic shots from the high peaks, but also insure that both the river and sky will appear in photos of the deep canyons.

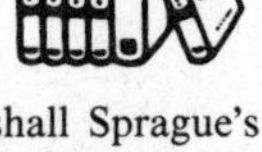

RECOMMENDED READING. Robert Brown's *Colorado Ghost Towns* will give insight into some of the ways of the Old West; *Timberline,* by Gene Fowler, offers a delightful peek into the Denver of not-so-very-long ago; Marshall Sprague's *Colorado* examines the history of the state; *Stampede to Timberline,* by Muriel Sibell Wolle, tells of ghost towns and mining camps; *Skiing Colorado* looks into the ski areas and resorts. James Michener's novel *Centennial* casts a light on the history of the eastern part of the state. *The Complete Book of Mountain Sports* contains valuable advice to prospective climbers, hikers, backpackers, and winter sports people. An excellent paperback by S. Kaye, *Small People in Big Places,* focuses on children and how to explore Colorado with them.

INTRODUCTION TO COLORADO

Snow-flecked Peaks Beckon

by
CURTIS CASEWIT

Colorado has become sophisticated and cosmopolitan, but the state is still the West. Its beauty acts as a magnet for millions of tourists each year. The Mile-High State's popularity is underlined by the fact that the Visitor's Bureau may get 3,000 inquiries—several sacks of mail—in one day.

In summer, the Colorado mountains attract hikers and campers, rock climbers and photographers, Jeep clubs and backpackers from everywhere. Ski resorts become tennis ranches. Many come to the picture-book mountain villages for a rich cultural fare of theater, jazz and classical music, and other events that greet visitors from early spring deep into the following winter.

Colorado's renowned dry snow attracts more than a million skiers every year, generating millions of dollars at the state's three dozen ski areas. Indeed, no U.S. state or Canadian province has more major ski resorts than Colorado. Some of the ski centers, like Winter Park, for instance, are so well managed that experts travel to the state all the way from distant points such as New Zealand and Australia to study that facility's expertise.

Colorado's boom is legendary. Manufacturing and construction top the list, producing more than $7 billion a year. Agriculture and livestock are next, averaging about $2.9 billion. Tourism accounts for another $2 billion or so, contributing large sums in state tax revenues. On the average, the state has been host to around 360,000 convention delegates a year, bringing in almost $166 million in revenue annually. The one-time kingpin of Colorado's economy—mining and minerals—runs third with just over $2.3 billion, about half of which is produced by oil and gas.

Energy Is Fueling Growth

According to the experts, Colorado will continue to grow through the eighties, thanks to the energy industry. Major oil companies foresee a Colorado-based billion-dollar shale oil industry. In addition, petroleum and natural gas deposits turned out to be much larger than anticipated. Energy developers and high-technology manufacturing—especially the electronic chip producers headquartering in and around Denver—keep the state's economy growing faster than the national average. Unemployment meanwhile hovers at about half the U.S. norm.

"Colorado is a national hot spot," says a Denver real estate developer. "More people consider us as one of the last nice places to live. That will continue to draw both individuals and industry."

In summer, the state's flat eastern section is a fertile field with melons, asparagus, corn and other edibles that are sold at numerous roadside stands. (A host of fruits also abound on the western slope of the Colorado mountains.) Each year, the state's farmers export thousands of tons of wheat, sugar beets and potatoes. The state's corn-fed beef is justly famous.

During the past decade, Denver and her sister cities along the Rockies' eastern rise have enjoyed great growth—indeed, Denver is the West's headquarters for the nation's energy boom. The Mile-High

City's skyline boasts dozen of super-contemporary buildings, such as the Amoco Tower and Energy Plaza. The offices are occupied by oil firms and geologists who have flooded the area since the mid-1970s.

West of the state capital, in Golden, is the federal Solar Energy Research Institute and beyond it, deep in the mountains, lie the pilot projects for the nation's oil shale and synthetic fuels.

Cultural Boom

As some 50,000 people relocate here each year from New York, Dallas, Chicago, the state has become culturally alive. Denver's Symphony orchestra is housed in the Boettcher Concert Hall, one of the country's newest and most modern facilities. Boulder, just north of Denver, is home to the annual Colorado Shakespeare Festival, which draws thespians and spectators from all over the country. Central City, an old mining town, hosts world-famous operatic performers in summer; and Aspen offers series of classical music programs. Each summer, the community of Telluride sponsors an international film festival attended by cinema greats. Telluride also has a bluegrass and dance festival. Colorado visitors will find a profusion of galleries, theater groups, musical ensembles, and ballets, which are attracting greater national notice.

Highway System

The state's many facets are linked by one of the nation's best highway systems. Interstate 70 traverses east and west, through Denver and the Rockies. Four lanes of it tunnel through the mountains of Loveland Pass. Interstate 25 arches Colorado's north-south middle through Pueblo, Colorado Springs, Denver, and on in to Wyoming. Almost all of the 9,200 miles of state highways are maintained through the winter. (Exceptions: Independence Pass on State Highway 82 near Aspen and Trail Ridge Road through Rocky Mountain National Park, which are usually snowed shut from late fall through early June.)

In the southern part of the state, the excellent US 50 connects Lamar with Pueblo, Salida, Gunnison, and Montrose. US 60 crosses west from Walsenburg to Durango. Before venturing into the hills in winter, visitors should call the Colorado State Patrol's special report line at (303) 639-1111. Recorded information, updated as conditions change, reports in detail road conditions throughout the Colorado Rockies.

Even if roads are periodically closed, travel is still possible in the Rockies, thanks to the many small air carriers which ferry skiers and other visitors in and out of the high country the year round. To be sure, it is the airliner that provides the most compelling and meaningful sight of the Rockies—a jumbled mass of forests, crags, and snow-flecked peaks stretching to the horizon. The great expanse of Colorado, eighth in size among the states, and the vastness of its wilderness (national forests cover one-fifth of the area) are impressively evident to the airline traveler.

The state has 1,143 mountains rising to an altitude of at least 10,000 feet above sea level—and 1,000 are two miles high or more. Fifty-three often snow-crowned peaks towering above 14,000 feet give the state more than six times the mountain area of Switzerland. Six major national parks and national monuments, plus 32 state parks and state recreation areas, provide an unsurpassed variety of recreational opportunities to satisfy almost any outdoor appetite. Also, hundreds of thousands of acres of private land are available to Colorado adventurers who respect the rights of landowners.

GENERAL PRACTICAL INFORMATION FOR COLORADO

FACTS AND FIGURES. Colorado got its name from the Spanish for "red" or "muddy," referring to the Colorado River. Colorado's nicknames are *Centennial State* (because it entered the Union on August 1, 1876) and *Silver State.* The state flower is the Rocky Mountain columbine; state tree, the Colorado blue spruce; the state bird, the lark bunting; state animal, the Rocky Mountain bighorn sheep; the state motto is *Nil sine Numine* ("Nothing without Providence"); the state song is "Where the Columbines Grow." Colorado is in the mountain time zone. Its area is 104,247 sq. mi.; altitude, 3,350–14,431 ft. The state population (last estimate) is 2,755,300. Denver, Colorado's largest city, is the state capital.

The Continental Divide and the Rocky Mountains cut a north-south path down the center of Colorado, forming the headwaters of six great rivers and dividing the state into the flat eastern region of the Great Plains and the high plateaus and deep gorges of the west. The mountainous western area contains some of the highest peaks in the country as well as some of America's finest resort areas. Mining remains important. The state is a leading source of molybdenum, oil shale, and uranium.

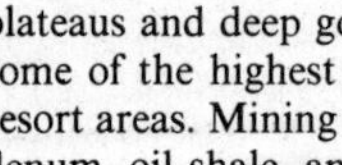

HOW TO GET THERE. By air: Colorado is served by *United, TWA, Eastern, Northwest Orient, U.S.Air, Ozark, Continental, Delta, American, Frontier, Texas International, Western, Republic, Mexicana, Piedmont*

and *Rocky Mountain* on regular schedules into Denver's Stapleton International Airport. Colorado Springs, Pueblo, and Grand Junction also have major service.

By train. *Amtrak* has passenger service into Denver originating in Chicago or San Francisco; Amtrak's *Southwest Limited* stops in Lamar, La Junta and Trinidad. Connecting service into Grand Junction is available from the Denver & Rio Grande Western Railway.

By car: Main highways into the state are I–25 from Wyoming in the north and New Mexico in the south; I–70 from Utah in the west and Kansas in the east; and I–80S from Nebraska in the northeast.

By bus. *Greyhound* and *Trailways* both serve Colorado.

HOW TO GET AROUND. By air: In addition to the major service into Denver, *Trans-Colorado, Frontier, Aspen Airways, Rocky Mountain,* and *United* provide air transportation within the state. Steamboat Springs-Hayden-Craig, Grand Junction. Aspen, Delta-Montrose, Gunnison, Cortez, Durango, Alamosa, Lamar, Pueblo, Eagle/Vail and Colorado Springs are all served by one or more of these airlines.

By train: *Denver & Rio Grande Western* operates passenger service between Denver and Grand Junction.

By bus: R.T.D., *Continental Trailways, Denver-Boulder R.T.D. Bus Company,* and *Greyhound* serve Colorado communities.

By car: The major east-west route is I–70; from north to south on the eastern slope take I–25, also known as the Valley Highway. US 550 serves the southwest corner, US 40 the northwest and US 50 and 160 cross southern Colorado.

CLIMATE. The climate allows a choice of activity in any season. While summer temperatures are quite high on Colorado's eastern prairies, the front-range cities are cooler and the weather seldom reaches the sweltering discomfort of America's more humid regions. Colorado's dry air seems lighter, and one can stroll, jog, or play tennis in relative comfort even as the mercury hits the 80s. Rains are rare along the foothills, but should be expected on some summer afternoons in the mountains. Throughout the state, evenings are cool. Bring a jacket and expect to sleep under blankets, especially at higher elevations.

Winters are as moderate as summers. The average January temperature is nearly 30° and the occasional snows melt in a day or two in the cities. Cold is tolerated easily in the dry air; in fact, many tennis resorts and outdoor swimming pools remain open all year. Nor is it unusual to see spring skiers wearing shorts or T-shirts on the slopes. Still, snows—light or heavy—are unpredictable. They may come well before Thanksgiving or not until Christmas. Plan your late fall or spring visits as though snowfalls could be a part of it.

Month	Average Daily Temperature Chart Max.	Min.	Ave.	Average Sunshiny Days	Average Precipitation	Average Humidity 11:30 A.M.
January	42.5	17.6	30.7	25	.47	.44
February	44.7	21.0	32.8	21	.85	.40
March	51.3	27.2	39.3	24	1.15	.35
April	60	35.6	47.7	23	1.61	.32
May	68.9	44.5	56.7	25	1.76	.30
June	80.5	53.5	66.8	26	1.46	.26
July	85.7	59.5	72.6	27	1.90	.27
August	84.3	58.3	71.3	26	1.77	.29
September	77	49.3	62.9	25	1.29	.29
October	64.6	38.4	51.5	26	1.12	.31
November	52.6	27.8	40.3	23	.76	.35
December	44.5	20.5	32.5	25	.78	.42
Yearly Averages and Totals	63.3	37.2	50.4	296	14.92	.33

ALTITUDE. Be sure to ease into Colorado's higher elevations. There is no doubt that a sudden stay at 7,000 to 13,000 feet above sea level will have an effect on the flatlander. At first you may tire a little and perhaps even feel lightheaded. Your skin becomes dry and requires supplementary moisture. And if you cook in the Colorado mountains, you'll notice that the 3-minute soft-boiled egg may take 4 to 5 minutes and that foods requiring 15 minutes' cooking need twenty or more.

In the sports world it is said that it takes one full day to get accustomed to 1,000 feet of altitude if you arrive from sea level. Certainly you should not engage in strenuous exercise on your first day here. Families might want to restrict their exertion during the first few days.

The same caveat applies to skiers, despite all the temptations of the high country: take a day to get used to the high, thin air.

Remember, too, that the air in the mountains is pure—no dust or other airborne matter is there to filter the sun. On a bright day, unprotected skin and lips can blister quickly. Bring suntan lotion; sunglasses are also helpful.

CAMPING OUT. Some six million people stay in Colorado's hundreds of campgrounds each summer. You can buy a pass to gain entrance to campsites at the many state-supervised outdoor areas; otherwise, there are also per-night fees. The same prices are found in the national parks. At both, check with rangers for camping regulations.

A "Golden Eagle" passport allows you and anyone in your vehicle to enter many national parks and recreational areas during a full calendar year. The passport doesn't cover all areas, nor does it include special fees. A "Golden Age" passport provides free park access to anyone 62 years of age or older. Blind or handicapped persons can also enjoy the "Golden Access" passport.

Information and applications are available from any office of the National Park Service, Forest Service, Bureau of Land Management, and at most ranger stations. Or you may write to National Park Service Headquarters, U.S. Department of the Interior, 18th and C Streets N.W., Washington, D.C. 20240.

Reservations can be made for campsites in state parks. Contact TeleCheck Minnesota, 5275 Edina Industrial Blvd., Edina, Minnesota 55435 (1-800-328-6338). $3 fee plus payment for 1 night required at least 15 days in advance.

At Rocky Mountain National Park, camping sites are scarce during the high summer season. However, you may get reservations on a first-come first-served basis, though not at Glacier Basin or Moraine Park; the latter may be reserved up to 8 weeks in advance for the peak summer season.

Many of Colorado's privately-owned campgrounds offer thousands of vehicle and tent sites in the state.

GUEST AND DUDE RANCHES. Colorado's wilderness can also be enjoyed by vacationing at four dozen dude ranches. All of them emphasize horseback riding, but some ranches also feature swimming pools and tennis courts. Fishing in mountain streams is popular as well.

Some are working cattle ranches where visitors become cowhands. All offer comfortable cabins, cookouts, and horseback riding aplenty—from a guided beginner's ride to breakfast rides, steak cookouts at night to six-day pack trips through the wilderness. Children have their own supervised programs. Dude ranches are popular, so reservations should be made as far in advance as possible (never less than two months ahead). Costs range from $200 to $550 per person per week.

Beaver Village Guest Ranch at Winter Park (Box 43, 80482) on US 40, is a well-known working dude ranch. Activities run from supervised programs for youngsters, to tennis, square dancing, pool swimming, lake and stream fishing, and barbecues, as well as the usual ranch activities. The **Drowsy Water Ranch,** in Granby (zip code 80446), can be found in the same region. On Colorado State Hwy. #7, directly under Long's Peak, there beckons **The Long's Peak Inn and Guest Ranch** (not far from Estes Park), which has some of the state's most exciting scenery.

Winter Park's **Idlewild Dude and Guest Ranch** (80482) provides outdoor tennis courts, while the **Sitzmark Ranch** (80482), not far away, is known for the personal attention of its owner. The **C Lazy U Ranch** (80446) near Granby has a long reputation for luxurious facilities and programs around the seasons. Also located in the mountains, the **Peaceful Valley Ranch,** Lyons (Star Route, 80540), made a name for itself as a riding center. It is the only such Colorado ranch which also specializes in square dancing.

In south-central Colorado, on State 96 west of Pueblo, the **Don K Ranch** (2677 S. Siloam Rd., 81005) boasts its own small ghost town. With the San Isabel Forest and the Sangre de Cristo Range to prowl, good food, heated pool, cocktail lounge, children's counselors, this may be the place for your Colorado vacation.

Other well known Colorado Ranches: **The Devil's Thumb Ranch** near Fraser (80442) doubles as a cross-country ski center in winter. The **Vista Verde Ranch** in Steamboat Springs (80477) has hunting in fall and sleigh rides in winter. Each ranch has its own character and diversions, but all feature horses. For more information, write Colorado Guest and Dude Ranch Association, Evergreen, CO 80439.

HIKING, BACKPACKING, RAFTING. More seasoned outdoorspeople may want to try the **hiking** trails that honeycomb the high country. The Colorado Mountain Club, 2530 W. Alameda Ave., Denver, Colo. 80219, publishes several guides to hiking trails on all levels of difficulty. The club also sponsors regular hikes and rock-climbing adventures. Guests are welcome for a small daily fee.

Backpackers should be prepared with both warm and cool clothing, crepe- or Vibram-soled shoes (impervious to sharp-edged rocks), a frame pack that centers your weight on hips instead of shoulders, and a first-aid kit. When trekking through government-supervised areas, you are required to sign in and out and let rangers know the general direction you're heading and roughly when you expect to return.

Those who tire of walking can go **rafting.** Guided river trips are available, lasting from a half-day to three weeks. River adventures vary in intensity, depending on whether you go along for the ride or grab an oar and wrestle the current yourself. Reservations, often a month or more ahead, are essential during the summer months. If you are experienced and prefer to go on your own, several outfitters rent rafts. Some stretches of river are open to raft-riders by permit only. Check locally.

HUNTING AND FISHING. Colorado is one of America's most popular **hunting** regions. Big game animals include the deer (mule and whitetail), elk, bear, mountain lion, bighorn sheep, and the Rocky Mountain goat.

Regular elk and deer seasons open in October. The antelope season starts in September and bighorn sheep and mountain goat seasons begin in late August. Special archery, muzzleloading and high-country deer and elk periods usually start prior to the regular deer and elk rifle seasons. Black bear may be hunted during the spring and summer and again during the state's regular big game seasons. The period for hunting mountain lion runs concurrently with the regular big game dates.

Residents and nonresidents may bag all species of big game animals except bighorn sheep and Rocky Mountain goat. The shooting of these two species is limited to Colorado residents only.

All regular big game licenses may be bought from authorized license agents, i.e., most of the state's hardware and sporting goods stores. It is true that the

Colorado Wildlife Commission may insist that you get your deer and elk licenses at Division of Wildlife offices after the opening of the regular rifle seasons. Licenses for specified and antlerless deer and elk hunting, for bighorn sheep, mountain goat, and antelope hunting are issued by application and drawing. The latter are usually available after the first of May each year.

Printed regulations on deer, elk, bear, and mountain lion seasons may be obtained after the first of August each year. Archery regulations are available in late May.

Guides are not required by law for big game hunting. But hunters unfamiliar with Colorado's more rugged mountains would be wise to use guide services, especially for elk hunting. A list of licensed guides and outfitters is published in July of each year by the Division (6060 Broadway, Denver, Colo. 80216).

Fishing, equally popular, extends to some 11,300 miles of mountain streams and most of Colorado's 2,400 lakes. Each spring and early summer the state stocks the lakes and many rivers with more than a million pounds of trout. Colorado's fishing season runs almost the year round with varying exceptions. Nonresident licenses are good for the balance of the calendar year in which they're purchased. Nonresident licenses for ten days are available, as are 2-day permits for $7. Licenses are sold through many hardware and outdoor-equipment shops. Ask for the Colorado Division of Wildlife's booklet on current fishing regulations, or write the Division for a copy at 6060 Broadway, Denver, Colo. 80216.

Naturally, the farther away you get from Denver, the better the fishing . . . especially if you can hike away from the main roads and know the wilderness.

Among Colorado's most widely known trout streams are the Gunnison, down to the Blue Mesa Reservoir; the Rio Grande, through the San Luis Valley and above it; the Arkansas, from below Leadville to Pueblo; the entire stretch of the Colorado, White, Yampa, North Platte rivers and the South Platte above Waterton south of Denver.

Some of the more popular trout lakes are Grand Lake at the town of Grand Lake; Granby and Shadow Mountain reservoirs near Granby; Dillon Reservoir near Dillon; Trappers Lake east of Meeker; Sweetwater Lake near Glenwood Springs; Twin Lakes near Leadville; Monument Lake near Trinidad; Vallecito Reservoir near Durango; lakes of the Grand Mesa near Grand Junction.

Other popular trout lakes are Delaney Butte Lakes and Lake John near Walden; the Red Feather lakes northwest of Fort Collins; Eleven Mile and Antero reservoirs in South Park; Taylor Reservoir near Gunnison; Williams Creek Reservoir near Pagosa Springs; Williams Fork Reservoir near Parshall; and Lon Hagler Reservoir near Loveland.

The relatively crowded waters of Dillon Reservoir at Dillon; Vega Reservoir near Colbran; Navajo Reservoir southwest of Pagosa Springs; and North Michigan Lake near Walden can all be of interest to trout anglers; ditto for the Blue Mesa Reservoir near Gunnison.

Near Denver, try the South Platte River from below the city to the town of Deckers; Bear Creek Lake, east of Morrison on US 285; or Cherry Creek Reservoir on the edge of southeast Denver.

NATIONAL PARKS AND MONUMENTS. The Black Canyon of the *Gunnison National Monument* is probably the deepest, darkest, wildest, and rockiest piece of real estate you will ever see. The Gunnison River has cut a narrow gorge, at times only forty feet wide, through nearly solid granite, to depths ranging from 1,730 feet to 2,425 feet. From the higher elevations it is possible to see the frothing white water below against a background of sunlight reflected from pink mica in the otherwise black walls. Legend has it that the canyon is so dark and narrow at the bottom that it is possible in broad daylight to see the stars by looking straight up. Well-organized boat trips down the river and descents on Indian trails may be taken, but only experienced climbers should attempt any other route down the canyon. Some of the best fishing in Colorado is to be found on the Gunnison. The North Rim of the canyon is reached by a gravel road east of Crawford on State 92. The South Rim is reached by US 50 to Montrose and then State Road, 347 six miles east. Park rangers have nightly programs during the summer. Campsites and picnic areas are available. Closed in winter by snow.

State 340 west from Grand Junction or US 70 from Fruita will lead into Rim Rock Drive of *Colorado National Monument,* 1,000 feet above the Grand Valley. Five-hundred-foot-high *Independence Rock, Window Rock,* the *coke ovens* and *Red Canyon* may be seen from lookouts along the 22-mile drive. Meadows of wildflowers and forests of juniper and pine surround the mountains. Wildlife, protected by the National Park Service, roam the area. Dinosaur beds are still being excavated here. Nearby, the largest flat-topped peak in the United States, *Grand Mesa,* sprinkled with lakes and two miles high, may be reached on State 64. The Visitors' Centers at park headquarters will assist the traveler in the area. Nightly programs by rangers during the summer. Campsites with excellent facilities and picnic areas are available. Well-marked trails beckon to hikers.

Dinosaur National Monument, in the northwestern corner of Colorado, is reached from US 40 at Dinosaur, park headquarters. Much of the scenic beauty is a result of erosion by the Yampa and Green rivers. *Steamboat Rock,* carved out of layers of sandstone by the confluence of the Yampa and Green is now seven hundred feet above the river surface which once flowed over it. Its broad slab sides act as a sounding board for nearby *Echo Park.* Pictographs estimated to be one thousand years old may be seen. Archeologists removed the delicate bones of dinosaurs from their sedimentary storehouses. More than twenty skeletons have been reconstructed here dating back some one hundred thousand years ago. The skeletons are housed in a museum reached through Jenson, Utah, twenty miles west of Dinosaur on US 40. Roads into the monument may be closed in winter due to snow. Campsites and raft trips are available in the region.

The only place in America where four states meet at one point is the junction of Arizona, New Mexico, Utah and Colorado. The area is locally called "The

Four Corners." *Hovenweep National Monument* is reached by a gravel park road west of Pleasant View, off State 666. The monument is a series of long-abandoned Pueblo settlements which punctuate the barren land and extend into southern Utah. The prehistoric buildings, evidently built by a people similar to those who built Mesa Verde, are open for inspection. A ranger is on duty at Square Tower. Campsites and picnic areas are available. In rainy or snowy weather check in Cortez before attempting the dirt road.

Mesa Verde National Park will doubtlessly impress the traveler. Just as fossils tell us how plants and animals lived long ago, the ruins of these cliff dwellings tell us of a prehistoric civilization from nearly a thousand years before the American Revolution.

It is believed that about eight hundred years ago land overuse, timber depletion, and overhunting forced the tribes that built Mesa Verde to leave their plateau for an area more favorable to them. Archaeologists and national park experts speculate that Mesa Verde's early inhabitants—now known as the *Anasazi*—were pueblo people. *Mesa Verde* ("Green Tabletop") describes the general topography of the surface of the park, not the caves and canyons below. There are three general types of ruins open for inspection. The *pithouses* are shallow holes in the ground, usually covered with straw or grass roofs, which were inhabited by one family. The pueblos form a village around the *kiva,* which was used for religious ceremonies. The *cliff dwellings* were built much later and offered excellent protection to their inhabitants. The *Cliff Palace* was built two hundred feet off the canyon floor and contains some two hundred rooms. The *Spruce Tree House* is relatively easy to enter and remains one of the best preserved. It has 114 rooms and eight *kivas* and is not unlike today's apartment houses. No one may enter the fragile cliff dwellings unless accompanied by a park ranger.

The museum at Park Headquarters will add to the visitor's understanding of Mesa Verde and her people. The park may be reached by car on US 160, 10 miles east of Cortez. Bus service from Spruce Tree Lodge is available for those who do not wish to drive their cars into the park; *Continental Trailways* has daily buses to Spruce Tree Lodge from Durango; bus service is also available from Cortez. *Frontier Airlines* serves Durango and Cortez ten miles west of Mesa Verde. A limited number of overnight accommodations are available at the *Far View Motor Lodge,* as are improved facilities for house trailers. A restaurant, service station, AAA road service, and tire agency exist. Evening campfire talks are given by park rangers and archeologists.

Rocky Mountain National Park, with headquarters at Estes Park, is scenically stunning. *Trail Ridge Road* (US 34), the highway which runs through part of the Park, has been called "breathtaking." The highest paved highway in the U.S., its fifteen miles of road above timberline, some at altitudes of twelve thousand feet, look down on great sloping meadows of wildflowers. Slowly melting glaciers provide the water supply for a host of waterfalls, streams, and deep mountain lakes. On *Long's Peak* (14,255 feet), snowballs can be made in the middle of July. At the western end of Trail Ridge Road is *Grand Lake,* which covers an area of 515 acres, and at 8,400 feet is the home of what may be the highest yacht club in the world. Water sports are popular here, but be prepared for the icy waters of a lake whose depths have never been completely sounded. And near the base of the Long's Peak Trail, you can inspect Enos Mills' old cabin, now a small museum for a Park pioneer, plus a nature trail.

Great Sand Dunes National Monument, located on State 150, thirty-six miles northeast of Alamosa, contains the highest naturally formed sand piles in the United States, some exceeding a height of eight hundred feet above the valley floor. The constant pressure of the wind sculpts the finely pulverized sand into a wonderland of hills, valleys, and plains. During the day the dunes can be visible for seventy miles, radiating a rosy warmth of sun on hot sand. The color and mood shift with the angle of the sun, as lengthening shadows change the dunes to violet and mauve. The dunes also produce some of the greatest lightning displays in America. The combination of wind and heat rising from the fifty-five square miles of sand creates titanic thunderstorms accompanied by extraordinary lightning bolts. The Visitors' Center contains history and information on the area; campsites and picnic grounds are available, and a nature trail is marked for hikers.

Florissant Fossil Beds National Monument, 35 miles west of Colorado Springs on U.S. 24, is a six thousand-acre site once covered by a prehistoric lake.

HOT SPRINGS. Colorado has a number of hot springs, among them *Glenwood Springs, Idaho Springs, Pagosa Springs, Hot Sulphur Springs,* and *Steamboat Springs,* most with facilities for enjoying the waters. Of these, Glenwood Springs is the most extensive, with two outdoor pools, one of them two blocks long. Open all year, these are fed by natural warm mineral waters. *Hot mineral baths* are available at the Vapor Cave Baths and Health Spa.

MUSEUMS AND GALLERIES. The *University of Colorado Museum* in Boulder is open to the public Mon. through Fri. The *Denver Museum of Natural History* is quite extensive. (Location: City Park, entrance fee). The *Denver Art Museum* is located on 14th Ave. Parkway W., on the south end of the Civic Center, and is accessible on many bus routes. Museum hours are Tuesdays through Saturdays, 10 A.M. to 4:30 P.M. (Wednesday evenings until 8 P.M.), and Sundays, 1 P.M. to 5 P.M. (entry fee).

Central City's Opera House is worth visiting. The Tabor Collection is housed in the *Gold Mine Museum.* Open daily.

The *Colorado Springs Fine Arts Center* and *Taylor Museum* offer an unusual collection of southwestern United States primitive folk art, American Indian art and contemporary works. The building itself is an unusual piece of architecture. The *Boulder Center For the Visual Arts* has changing contemporary art exhibitions. *Colorado Car Museum* stays open throughout the summer.

Hagans Clock Manor Museum near Evergreen features a collection of clocks and music boxes. Guided tours, lectures, films, and programs.

The *Hotel De Paris* and the *Hamill House,* both in Georgetown, contain Victorian furnishings and architecture. Both these museums are open daily in the summer, and both charge a small fee.

Children are welcome in the *Buffalo Bill Museum* on *Lookout Mountain,* which contains items dealing with Cody's life and associates. Open daily. Free.

The *Colorado School of Mines* in Golden operates a geology museum for anyone interested in minerals, fossils, rock, or ores. The *Colorado Railroad Museum,* with the largest railroad display in the Rockies, is housed in an 1880-style railroad station in Golden.

In Estes Park there is the *MacGregor Ranch Museum* preserving a century's worth of ranch history.

La Junta is the home of the *Koshare Indian Dancers* and their museum, located at *Otero Junior College.* This *Kiva* contains Indian art, handicrafts, and lore. Open all year. In Aspen, meanwhile, the *Aspen Historical Society Museum* focuses on miners, settlers and skiers.

The Colorado Ski Museum and Hall of Fame in Vail has some unique historic exhibits of interest to skiers.

H. A. W. Tabor left his mark on Colorado's culture. Leadville preserved and restored his last mine and the opera house he built for the town. Both the *Matchless Mine* and the *Tabor Opera House* are worth seeing. Tabor also built the opera house in Central City, used in summer as a theater and opera house. The small Heritage Museum in Leadville is also worth a visit. (Closed in winter.)

The *Sangre de Cristo Arts Center* in Pueblo is a large, new complex with galleries, theater, and dance.

Trinidad offers the *Baca House* and the *Bloom Mansion* for public visits. The Baca House is an 1869 adobe residence; the Bloom Mansion is the 1882 baroque Victorian residence of a local cattle baron.

Numerous towns in Colorado have a museum of some sort. The state historical society maintains a number of forts, monuments, residences, and sites throughout the state.

HISTORIC SITES. *Old Fort Garland,* on US 160, forty-seven miles west of Walsenburg, is a restored Army post that was once commanded by Kit Carson. On US 85 south of Platteville is a reproduction of *Fort Vasquez,* a fur-trading post of the 1830s. *Pike's Stockade,* a moated log structure built in 1807 by Zebulon Pike, is on US 285 east of La Jara. Buffalo Bill Cody's grave is atop Lookout Mountain, west of Denver on US 40.

Mining played an important part in Colorado's history, and more than three hundred *ghost towns* still survive today as remnants of the state's legendary past. The Central City-Black Hawk area was once known as the "richest square mile on earth," and the ghost towns of Nevadaville and Apex, and Central City's *Teller House* and *1878 Opera House* are reminders of the mining that came and went. The "world's greatest gold camp" was at Cripple Creek-Victor, where several excellent ghost towns survive. At the edge of Fairplay, one of Colorado's oldest cities, the 100-year-old town of South Park City has been reconstructed.

SPECIAL INTEREST TOURS. The Durango to Silverton narrow-gauge railroad passes through spectacular Rocky Mountain scenery. First built in 1882 principally to carry precious metals out of the area. Now a tourist rail line, it still uses steam locomotives. The train leaves Durango every summer morning and arrives at Silverton at noon. The return trip leaves Silverton in the afternoon and reaches Durango before supper. Trains run daily from late May to early Oct. and during certain winter days (inquire at Depot). Enjoyable, especially for children, but don't wear your best clothes for this excursion.

ENTERTAINMENT. The Broadmoor Hotel in Colorado Springs brings in "name" entertainment, particularly to their *Broadmoor International Theatre.* During the ski season, both Aspen and Steamboat Springs feature some nightclub activity.

BARS. Colorado's best bars are interesting in their own right. *The Golden Bee,* at the Broadmoor Hotel in Colorado Springs, is an authentic replica of a 19th-century English pub. Central City boasts a wide variety of Old West drinking places. The famous "Face on the Barroom Floor" is in the bar at *Teller House.*

DRINKING LAWS. Colorado Law requires that anyone purchasing hard liquor, wine, or "6%" beer must be *21 years of age.* Persons over 18 may purchase so-called "3.2" beer. Drinks must be off the table at closing hour. Package goods are not sold in the bar, but may be obtained in package stores, open until midnight, Mon. through Sat. Children may sit at a table if they are accompanied by an adult. In recent years, the state has added stiff drunk driving laws.

MUSIC. Tops among the many musical activities outside of Denver is the *Aspen Music Festival,* held each summer with nationally known artists. Likewise, there are classical concerts in Vail; moreover, the Denver Symphony Orchestra travels to other resorts and towns. Many large Colorado cities and towns have local orchestras and bands which perform throughout the year, and the many colleges and universities in the state all feature musical events throughout the school term. For example, Fort Collins' Lincoln Center hosts ballets, opera, and other music. Mid-June through July sees the *Boulder Music Festival.* Summer opera exists in Colorado Springs. Music lovers drive south to Santa Fe, N.M., in summer for more fine opera. The Pueblo Symphony has become known, too, particularly for its soloists.

STAGE AND REVUES. Boulder has an important summer *Shakespeare Festival,* backed by an excellent *University Theater* group. Other colleges and universities throughout the state have student theaters and often bring in outside talent to perform. Various towns throughout the state have melodramas which are presented Wild West style, with much hissing at the villains and cheering of the heroes. Among the state's best known are the melodramas at the Imperial Hotel (Cripple Creek), the *Country Music Theatre* of Estes Park, offer performances throughout the year. At Steamboat Springs, the *Steamboat Repertory Theatre* presents drama almost all year. Closer to Denver, in Golden, *The Heritage Square Opera House* goes in for boisterous western melodramas. Colorado Springs has a summer opera season.

SPECTATOR SPORTS. Auto racing: the famous Pikes Peak Hill Climb takes place July 4th outside Colorado Springs and, at the Continental Divide Raceways in Castle Rock, there is stock and sports car racing from May to Sept. **Greyhound racing:** from late Mar. to early June at the Cloverleaf Kennel Club in Loveland, from early June to mid-Aug. at Pueblo Kennel Association in Pueblo, and during Sept. and Oct. at Rocky Mountain Kennel Club. **Horse racing:** at the Centennial Race Track in Littleton (February through November). **Rodeo:** although many communities have rodeos, some of the best known are the "Pikes Peak or Bust Rodeo" in Colorado Springs during the second week in Aug., and the Colorado State Fair and Rodeo in Pueblo beginning late Aug. Others take place at Craig, Montrose, Estes Park, Salida, Gunnison, Loveland, Canon City, Steamboat Springs, Boulder, Monte Vista, and Glenwood Springs.

SHOPPING. Colorado has more than its share of ordinary curio shops and souvenir counters, but it also provides some different and interesting shops. Aspen's sports shops are always reliable; browsers will also enjoy the Keystone Resort, Winter Park (in summer or winter) or Breckenridge. Colorado Springs' *Broadmoor Hotel* features a number of elegant boutiques. The state is best known for its skis, ski wear and mountaineering items.

WHAT TO DO WITH THE CHILDREN. Children in Colorado can find activities of all kinds and types to keep them busy. The *Cheyenne Mountain Zoo* in Colorado Springs will delight them. The *North Pole,* northwest of Colorado Springs, is the home of Santa's Workshop. A Wild West stagecoach, miniature train, Santa's car, and a magic-mine ride, plus doll-makers, puppeteers, magicians, glassblowers, and shops all make for enjoyment. The *Ghost Town Museum,* in Colorado Springs, caters to the imaginations of adults and children alike. The national forests and monuments are made to order for children who love the outdoors, but it would be well to warn them about wandering off alone. The old mining towns, especially Central City and Leadville, will offer dozens of places for browsing, looking, and learning. Abandoned mines should not be entered, since the timbers are dry and could collapse, but many old mines have been safety-checked and may be entered with a guide, usually for a small fee. The *Garden of the Gods* and *Cave of the Winds,* both near Colorado Springs, offer unusual sights. Manitou Springs has a car museum. Wonderful for a day's excursion is the *Cumbres & Toltec Scenic Railroad* from Antonito, Colorado, and Chama, New Mexico. Throughout the state, there are several nature trails, notably on *Lookout Mountain* in the Golden foothills.

INDIANS. Colorado's history is inextricably bound to Indian culture and lore. Today the state has two reservations, the *Ute Mountain* and *The Southern Ute Reservations,* in southwestern Colorado. The Mountain Utes, while clinging to many ancestral traditions, have modern conveniences. Each summer the Utes stage their traditional *Sun Dance.* Visitors are welcome, but cameras are not allowed. The Southern Utes hold their *Bear Dance* near Ignacio in May. In July, the Koshare Indian Dancers gather for summer festivities in La Junta; December sees the Dancers here for a winter night ceremonial.

SEASONAL COLORADO EVENTS. In **January,** is the *Winterskol Carnival* in Aspen and *ski races* throughout the state. Winter Park holds its annual *Winter Carnival* at the end of the month. Steamboat Springs, Leadville, and Crested Butte host *winter carnivals* in **February,** several ski races, downhill and slalom, take place in Aspen, and Georgetown celebrates *Fasching,* nine days of German festivities at mid-month.

March brings *torchlight parades* and *cutter races* to Steamboat Springs, *ski races* to various areas, and the *U.S. National Men's Curling Championships* to the Broadmoor World Arena in Colorado Springs.

The *Estes Park Hobby Show* and *Boulder Symphony Spring Concerts* open in **April.** *Easter Sunrise Services* take place at the Garden of the Gods near Colorado Springs, as well as in the Red Rocks Park near Morrison.

May events include statewide *rodeos, horse racing, golf tournaments,* Canon City's *Blossom Festival,* the *opening of Trail Ridge Road,* Basin's *May Day Slalom,* the Alamosa Rail Fan Club's annual *narrow-gauge railroad trip,* and *horse shows* throughout the state.

Melodramas open in **June** in Cripple Creek, Durango, and various other towns; there are *June Week and Graduation* ceremonies at the United States Air Force Academy in Colorado Springs. Grand Lake's *Sunrise Slalom,* Central City's *Opera and Drama Festival, waterskiing* tournaments, and the *Arkansas River International White Water Boat Race* at Salida. *Strawberry Days* in Glenwood Springs.

In June, Aspen holds an important yearly *International Design Conference.* And Aspen's *Music Festival* usually begins in late June and runs through mid-August. The *Renaissance Festival* beckons in Larkspur the first weekend in June and runs every weekend through mid-July. Winter Park opens its *Summer Alpine Slide* and *hiking programs.*

July means *stockcar races, rodeos* (Steamboat Springs) and *horse shows* including the *National Arabian Horse Show* at Estes Park. Fourth of July activities abound, among them: the *Pikes Peak Hill Climb and auto race;* Winter Parks holds its "Alpine Art Affair"—an arts and crafts festival, and the annual *Rotary Fireworks* take place in Gunnison. *Copper Mountain's Special Celebration,* complete with classical music, barbecues and foot races. Grand Lake has a *buffalo barbecue;* Boulder's *Shakespeare Festival* opens in Mary Rippon Theater; the "world's highest, longest, roughest, and toughest" race, the *Pack Burro Championship Race* over Hoosier Pass, takes place between Fairplay and Breckenridge; and the *Broadmoor International Theatre* at the Broadmoor Hotel in Colorado Springs imports name entertainers through August. One of the most popular events—the *Jazz Festival*—takes place in Telluride. Mid-July is also the time for Gunnison's annual *Cattlemen's Days Celebration.*

In **August,** Grand Junction offers the *Intermountain Market Days;* Alamosa stages a *Kit Carson Riders Futurity Race and Derby;* Grand Lake has the *Sailboat Regatta;* Littleton holds the *National Little Britches Rodeo Finals;* the *Colorado State Fair* takes place at Pueblo; the *Pikes Peak or Bust Rodeo* is at Colorado Springs; and the *Navajo Trail Festival* in Durango includes a rodeo, square dancing, parade, and horse racing. *Melon Day* is in Rocky Ford, in the Arkansas valley.

The University of Colorado's *football* season begins in **September.** Glenwood Springs has its annual *Art Festival,* and *Aspencades,* trips into the mountains to see the colorful changes autumn brings to the aspens; *rodeos* and *harvest festivals* are also common. On Labor Day, the *Garfield County Fair and Rodeo* takes place in Rifle. And in Vail, there is the yearly *Jerry Ford International Golf Tournament.*

October: *Potato Day* in Glenwood Springs, the *Stone Age Fair* in Loveland, and the opening of the *big-game hunting* season.

Most of the state's thirty-four *ski areas open* in **November.** *Goose hunting* season opens.

Hockey season begins at the World Arena in Colorado Springs in **December.** Georgetown, the mountain town, has an old-fashioned market then; on New Year's Eve is the Ad Am An *fireworks display* on Pikes Peak.

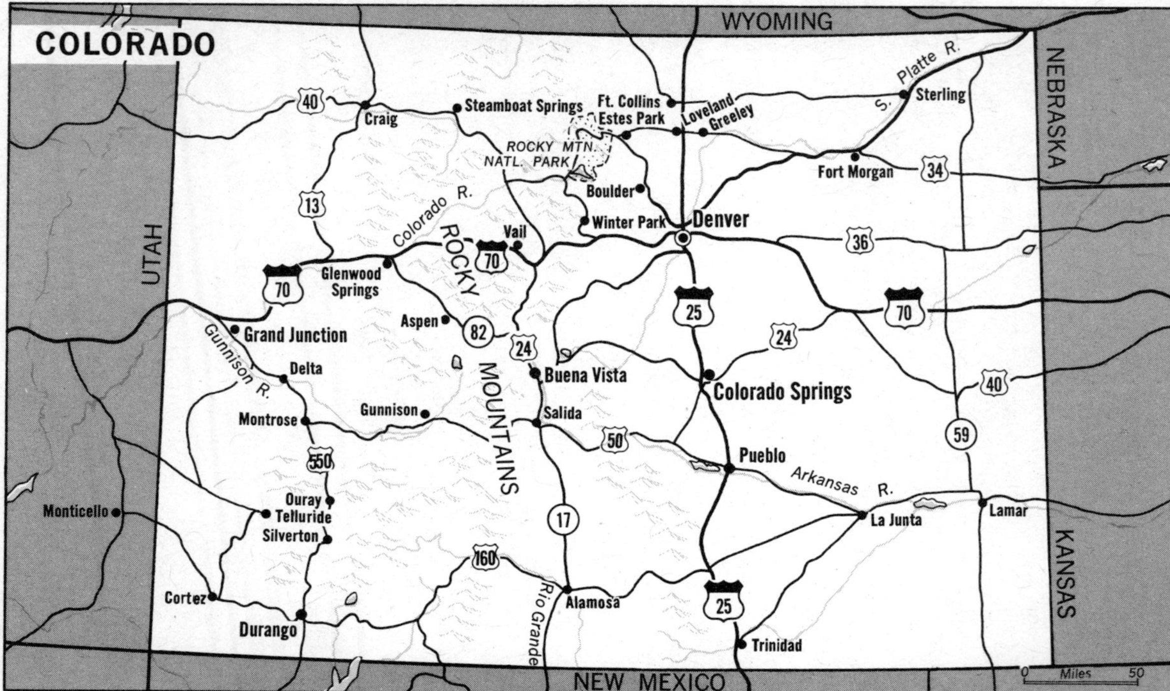
COLORADO
WYOMING
NEBRASKA
KANSAS
NEW MEXICO
UTAH
Craig
Steamboat Springs
Ft. Collins
Estes Park
Loveland
Greeley
Sterling
S. Platte R.
ROCKY MTN. NATL. PARK
Fort Morgan
Boulder
Winter Park
Denver
Colorado R.
Vail
ROCKY
MOUNTAINS
Glenwood Springs
Aspen
Grand Junction
Gunnison R.
Delta
Buena Vista
Colorado Springs
Gunnison
Montrose
Salida
Pueblo
Arkansas R.
Ouray
Telluride
Silverton
Monticello
La Junta
Lamar
Alamosa
Rio Grande
Cortez
Durango
Trinidad
40
13
70
82
24
25
36
34
59
50
550
17
160
0 Miles 50

THE HISTORY OF COLORADO

The Shining Mountains

Struggling westward across the Great Plains more than a century ago, a now-forgotten pioneer at the head of a wagon train gazed at the Colorado Rockies in the far distance. The morning sun glanced off the frosted peaks, vivid in the parched air, beckoning with a promise of green forests, cool waters, and gold.

"The Shining Mountains," the pioneer muttered, half in awe at their beauty, half in exasperation at the massive granite stretched across the horizon.

The sight was new to white settlers. But many humans had seen it long before. Folsom Man lived and hunted on the eastern plains 20,000 years ago. To mark his passing, he left well-fashioned stone arrowheads, spear points, and knives.

Four centuries before Columbus, cliff-dwelling Indians built and occupied multi-story apartment houses in the dry canyons of southwestern-most Colorado. No one is quite sure where they went, or why. The ruins of some of their homes are still preserved, most notably at Mesa Verde National Park, where visitors may stroll along ancient trails and ponder this lost civilization.

Less than a half century after Columbus stumbled on the New World—in 1541, to be exact—the Spaniard Coronado may have led an exploratory party north from Mexico in search of fabled Quivera and the Seven Cities of Cibola, where the streets were allegedly paved with gold. Coronado found no gold and no streets. The exact route of his march is unclear, but it is possible he cut across what is now southeastern Colorado.

Colorado's earliest European influence came with the Spaniards who established outposts north of Mexico as early as 1610. Tree rings tested from old mineshaft timbers also suggest dates from the early 1700s. And the town of La Plata, or "silver," was named for the area where Juan Maria de Rivera found huge deposits of the metal in 1765.

The Spanish left their language throughout Colorado. Streets are named Mariposa ("butterfly") and Tejon, pronounced tay-HOHN, meaning "badger". There are the San Juan and Sangre de Cristo mountains, towns such as Pueblo. Many descendants of early Spanish settlers now hold important posts in industry and state government.

As early as 1700, French voyagers pushed into the Rockies in search of furs. During the following century or so, they left behind such durable names as Cache la Poudre for the river on whose banks they hid their surplus gunpowder. And the same year that a doughty bunch of discontented colonists assembled in Philadelphia to declare their independence from England, Escalante and Dominguez, two Spanish friars in long robes, hiked from Santa Fe to the region of northwest Colorado before heading west.

Explorers, then Trappers

Colorado was largely an uncharted and unknown wasteland when it became U.S. property under the Louisiana Purchase in 1803. Shortly thereafter President Jefferson ordered Lieutenant Zebulon M. Pike to investigate the area he had bought. Late in 1806 Pike reached the foot of the 14,110-foot peak named in his honor. An intrepid explorer but no mountain climber, Pike duly noted in his official report that it was unlikely the summit would ever be scaled. Each summer now, tens of thousands of visitors reach the peak in comfort via automobile or a cog railway. And members of the Ad Am An Club, which gets it name from the fact it takes in a member each year, hike up Pikes Peak each New

Year's Eve to shoot off fireworks trucked up before snow closes the highway.

Pike's party missed quite a sight. In 1893 a Wellesley College English professor, Katherine Lee Bates, was enjoying the view from the peak when the words that became "America the Beautiful" began to take shape in her head. "Oh, beautiful for spacious skies, for amber waves of grain," she wrote. "For purple mountain majesties above the fruited plain."

The trek to the farmlands of the Northwest, the Mormon migration to Utah, and the 1849 California Gold Rush largely bypassed Colorado.

The land that had been ignored was to have its day. In 1858 Green Russell, a Georgia prospector married to a Cherokee Indian, found small amounts of placer gold on the banks of Cherry Creek where Denver now stands. That same year, gold was also discovered near Dry Creek, in what is now the Denver suburb of Englewood. With memories of the California gold rush still fresh, fortune-hunters scrambled west to stake the likeliest claims. These finds also drew financiers and entrepreneurs of every kind. Now it was "Pikes Peak or Bust," and many of the tenderfoot miners did go bust, for the sands were not nearly so rich as had been supposed. The hungry and disillusioned headed back to "the States," grumbling about the "Pikes Peak hoax." The hardy stuck it out and were rewarded in the spring of 1859 when John Gregory discovered rich gold deposits in a steep gulch forty miles west of the Cherry Creek settlements. This was to become the site of the twin towns of Central City and Blackhawk, called "the richest square mile on earth" until that title was wrested away thirty years later by another Colorado mining district, Cripple Creek.

Horace Greeley, then editor of the *New York Tribune,* was among the first easterners to reach Gregory's Gulch. He found some four thousand residents there, "including five white women and seven squaws living with white men." Half of the men had arrived within the week, with five hundred more coming in daily. Greeley reported everyone slept "in tents or under booths of pine boughs, cooking and eating in the open air." He wrote that there was gold to be found. Soon prospectors were pushing into the most isolated alpine valleys, washing the sands for gold, scarring the hillsides with their drilled holes.

When the gold played out, silver replaced it. Railroads and the cattle industry guaranteed Denver's place as the hub of the West.

The city also owes much to General William Larimer, often credited as Denver's founder. His log cabin, built in 1858 at what has become the downtown intersection of 15th and Larimer streets, was one of the town's first. (Nearly everyone else lived in tents.) Although the front door was made from an old coffin lid, his place was Denver's first to have a genuine glass window. It was Larimer who jumped the claim of an older "town corporation" across the Platte River and named the resulting settlement "Denver City" in honor of the territorial governor, General James W. Denver.

In the city's infancy, anyone could win title to two lots by building a sixteen-foot-square cabin astride them. The enterprise of Parkinson, Thompson, and Mickey maintained a staff of scouts, both in the city and out, and a warehouse full of prefabricated tin shacks. If any settler left his land for any length of time before his cabin was finished, he was likely to find a PT&M shack on it—complete with well-armed "residents"—when he returned. When enough citizens tired of being robbed, Parkinson, Thompson, and Mickey were run out of town.

Diversion from the sometimes brutal facts of frontier life was provided by the infamous "Market Street Row" of saloons, sporting houses, and other dens of leisure. The bigger houses were draped with velvet and lined with rosewood furniture from the East. A lavish reception at such a place was grounds enough to postpone courtroom trials or city council meetings. Some of the more colorful proprietors—such as Mattie Silks, who carried a pearl-handled revolver in the pocket of her Medici-style gowns—became politically powerful as well as famous. However, Victorian morality made its way to Denver just as the settlers had, and the Row was legislated closed in 1915. Many of the buildings, now faded and stripped of their opulence, may still be seen along Market Street on the edge of downtown.

The West's rich gold and silver finds sped up construction all over the territory. But the steep terrain and the need for many switchback curves all devoured the builder's funds. In Colorado, some companies financially bit off more than they could chew and went bankrupt. Other enterpreneurs accumulated fortunes with toll roads across the mountains. Business could be brisk in the Rockies. Marshall Sprague, a Western writer, describes the way to Leadville, Colorado, when thousands streamed across the Divide in 1878, as "jammed with wagons, stages, buggies, carts. There were men pushing wheelbarrows, men riding animals, men and dogs driving herds of cattle, sheep, pigs and goats."

Transportation Mishaps

Most of the area's stagecoach traffic would slow down in winter. Travel across the Continental Divide's "High Line Road" was always fraught with hazards. The six-horse teams would get stuck in the snow up to their bellies, and it was not unusual for the sleighs to topple over, catapulting their human cargo into a soft snowbank. The teamsters wore long overcoats and burlap sacks to keep warm. In summer, the stage line promised "No walking, no dust, no danger." But storms and rains could rut road coils over the Divide. Things could get so bad that drivers had to put planks across the washed-out or potholed road sections. Between present-day Dillon and Georgetown, Colorado, some stages had to turn back altogether.

At this time, the rails had been laid in many high places, too, and trains ran along some hair-raising mountain shelves. Thanks to mining riches, there was frequent discussion about an "Atlantic-Pacific" tunnel to be built with convict labor through the Divide. Nothing came of it, but a unique idea was hatched by W.A.H. Loveland, who'd built the original High Line Road, and for whom Colorado's Loveland Pass was eventually named.

The financier wanted to build nothing less than a railroad across the mountainous hurdle. And why not? Loveland had organized the Colorado Central Railroad, and one of his tracks ran from Denver to Georgetown, some miles short of the Pass. Should there not be an extension to Utah and the Pacific? Unfortunately, Loveland's scheme faced some unexpected obstacles. Trouble began when the residents of a mountain hamlet mobbed the Chinese railroad laborers. The Chinese crew fled in terror. Other workers found the laying of rails—and the climate—too rough for their liking, and many of them quit. Besides, there was the problem of ferrying the tracks across the inhospitable Continental Divide. The resourceful W.A.H. Loveland planned to use buckets and haul the rails over the ridges by cable. Eventually, his money ran out, and the project was abandoned. In the meantime, though, the Union Pacific trains were running across the Divide in Wyoming and other states. By 1885, the Canadian Pacific spanned the Rockies to the north.

Colorado's growth was swift and hectic. On February 28, 1861, Congress approved a bill to establish Colorado Territory, and Colonel William Gilpin, a hero of the Mexican War, was appointed governor. The population at that time was established by a not altogether reliable census at 20,798 white males, 4,484 white females and 89 native to the territory—Cheyenne, Arapaho, Comanche and Kiowa on the eastern plains, the Utes in the western mountains. When gold was discovered, more and more whites moved west, under the protection of Federal troops. As the Indians were displaced, there were armed disputes between various tribes and the Federal troops.

Young as it was, Colorado Territory had a key role in the Civil War. A motley volunteer army, quickly organized by Governor Gilpin, marched south to meet a Confederate cavalry force moving up from Texas under General Henry H. Sibley. They met at Glorieta Pass in northern New Mexico. The charging calvary proved to be no match for the miner-army, whose marksmanship had been sharpened in the mountains. Sibley's force was shattered and the gold fields preserved for the Union. Had the Confederacy seized Colorado gold, Jefferson Davis might have been able to shore up the South's economy.

Colorado derives its nickname, "The Centennial State," from the fact that it became a state one hundred years after the signing of the Declaration of Independence. It was the thirty-eighth state.

Nowhere is the spirit of early Coloradans illustrated more dramatically than in the railroads they built—narrow-gauge lines that wound up and up over prohibitive grades into areas where the Iron Horse had no business. Reaching far above timberline, operators of these lines faced crushing winter maintenance problems. Still, thanks to these railroads, inaccessible areas were eventually opened for development, mining was made feasible, towns were supplied and the state stitched together. Some of these lines have been converted to standard gauge, but most, alas, have been abandoned as mining dwindled or trucks took over.

In 1902, David H. Moffat, a Denver banker, organized a railroad to drive straight over the Rockies to the Pacific Coast. Corona Pass broke the railroad's back. The Continental Divide at this point is 11,680 feet above sea level. Winter storms made it impossible to maintain schedules. Finally, in 1922, the State Legislature passed a measure setting up the Moffat Tunnel Improvement District. Bonds were issued and work started on a tunnel under the Divide. The bore is six miles long, took five years to complete, and cost $18 million. The tunnel finally gave Denver direct access to the sea. The old roadbed over Corona Pass is open in summer to adventurous motorists willing to brave chuckholes, sharp curves and dust. The views are magnificent.

Gold and silver spurred that state's growth in the decades after statehood. Great silver strikes in Leadville, Aspen, and Creede produced millions in new wealth. Between 1880 and 1890 Colorado's population doubled to 413,000. Then came the repeal of the Sherman Act in 1893, slashing the price of silver. Mines ceased operations, and town died overnight.

During this black period only the Cripple Creek gold fields kept the state's economy afloat. Discovered in 1890, this area just southwest of Pikes Peak produced some $400 million worth of gold before the richest lodes were played out. Texas Guinan began her career as an entertainer in Cripple Creek. Lowell Thomas spent his boyhood there. Jack Dempsey worked in its mines and fought for a $50 purse. Only summer tourists keep Cripple Creek alive today, but the proposed reopening of the long-fallow mines may change the community's economy in the near future.

As mining dwindled, Coloradans realized their real wealth lay elsewhere. Farming grew as irrigation projects made more water available.

Mountain pastures fattened growing herds of cattle and sheep. Manufacturing plants were established in some cities. At Pueblo, coal from Trinidad was used to smelt ores from Leadville. The now giant C.F.&I. Steel Corporation took shape here. Mining equipment firms, first established to meet local needs, began to ship their specialized machinery to South America, Europe, and Asia.

Meanwhile, the population grew steadily, even during the dust bowl years of the thirties when drought and wind devastated the southeastern corner of the state. Colorado's population topped one million for the first time in the 1930 census and boomed after World War II. Now almost 2.8 million people live in the state.

The Soldiers Came Back

Three out of four Coloradans live in a corridor of cities stretched along the eastern foot of the Rockies, with Denver in the center. In fact, Grand Junction and Durango are the only communities west of the Divide to claim more than 10,000 residents. An estimated 1.6 million—more than half of all Coloradans—live in the Denver metropolitan complex.

The Colorado of today is a far cry from the rowdy cattle country of a generation ago. Thousands of servicemen who had trained during World War II at Lowry Air Base in Denver, Fort Carson near Colorado Springs, and Camp Hale for mountain troops near Leadville, had fallen in love with the West, vowed to come back, and did. City-jaded Easterners sought and found breathing space in Colorado. Wealthy Texans bought into Colorado real estate, not without some hard feelings among fishermen who found favorite trout streams posted. Other new blood was attracted by the expansion of oil, research, and aerospace-oriented industries. These newcomers were responsible for profound changes in the state's intellectual climate and outlook.

The arrival of Palmer Hoyt from Portland, Ore., coincided with the population influx. As editor and publisher of *The Denver Post,* the state's largest newspaper, Hoyt was as responsible as anyone for jolting Colorado out of its traditional provincialism. Perhaps it is significant that Denver's airfield soon became an international airport, and that it has two sister cities, Brest, France, and Takayama, Japan. Moreover, Denver is now linked by direct flights to several European gateways. The state has always been popular with the Swiss, Austrians, and Germans, many of whom settled or visited here. Many ethnic groups have contributed to a state as rich as it is diverse.

Indeed, Colorado seems to have it all—a colorful past, energy, industry, a variety of lifestyles, and some of the world's pretty scenery. As

James Michener wrote in *Centennial,* "Colorado may be the best remainin' spot on earth."

EXPLORING DENVER AND ENVIRONS

Growing by Leaps and Bounds

Anyone who knew Denver in the early 1970s wouldn't recognize it today. The growing city with a small-town ambience has become a full-fledged metropolis.

Denver is the center of finance and commerce for the Southwest, the nation's fastest-growing region. Its population swells with arrivals from New York, Dallas, San Francisco and other capitals. The new families have reclaimed dilapidated downtown neighborhoods, such as historic Capitol Hill, restored the old brick and frame homes, and have made the area thrive again.

The new Denverites have brought with them their favorite shopping, dining, and entertainment from around the world. City stores offer wares from antique clothing to Oriental jade, computers, even Greek and Thai groceries. Lovers of *haute cuisine* will find their pleasure in scores of restaurants, such as the award-winning Quorum or the French Normandy, which rival or surpass standards set by prestigious restaurants of both U.S. coasts.

Indeed, the visitor to the Mile-High City can now find any ethnic dining experience: there are restaurants with an authentic French, German, Swiss, Italian, Spanish, Greek, Mexican, and assorted Oriental cooking. You even discover Afghan and Moroccan places. Denver's ethnic cuisine reflects its varied populace.

Thanks to a more and more sophisticated public, the Colorado state capital also excels in its cultural life. The Denver Symphony and the Denver Center Theater Company are now at home in ultra-modern performance halls in the heart of downtown. The Denver Art Museum regularly hosts top international exhibits. Foreign motion pictures garner large audiences. Denver is now rated among the more sophisticated cities in the U.S.

The Layout

The Mile-High City's thoroughfares are simply arranged: north/south streets and east/west avenues form a grid. Street addresses start in both directions from Broadway, avenue addresses from Ellsworth. Street names fall in alphabetical order west of Broadway and east of Colorado Boulevard.

In the heart of downtown Denver, thoroughfares run diagonally to the normal grid (see map). Numbered *streets* are in this section; the balance of the city has numbered *avenues.* (17th St., for instance, is immediately downtown—17th Ave. is not).

You can pick up assorted pamphlets from the city's **Visitors' Bureau** at 225 W. Colfax, just off the main business section and at the edge of the Civic Center complex. The center is directly across the street from City Hall (distinguishable by the clock tower and chimes), which Denverites call the City and County Building.

Downtown Highlights

The Denver Mint, 320 West Colfax, across from the Visitors' Bureau. A Denver branch of the U.S. Treasury opened at 16th and Market streets in 1862. But, due to "the hostilities of the Indian tribes along the routes," coinage didn't begin here until the present building was finished in 1906.

More than 5 billion coins are stamped here each year. The Mint is open for weekday tours all year, except the last two weeks in June

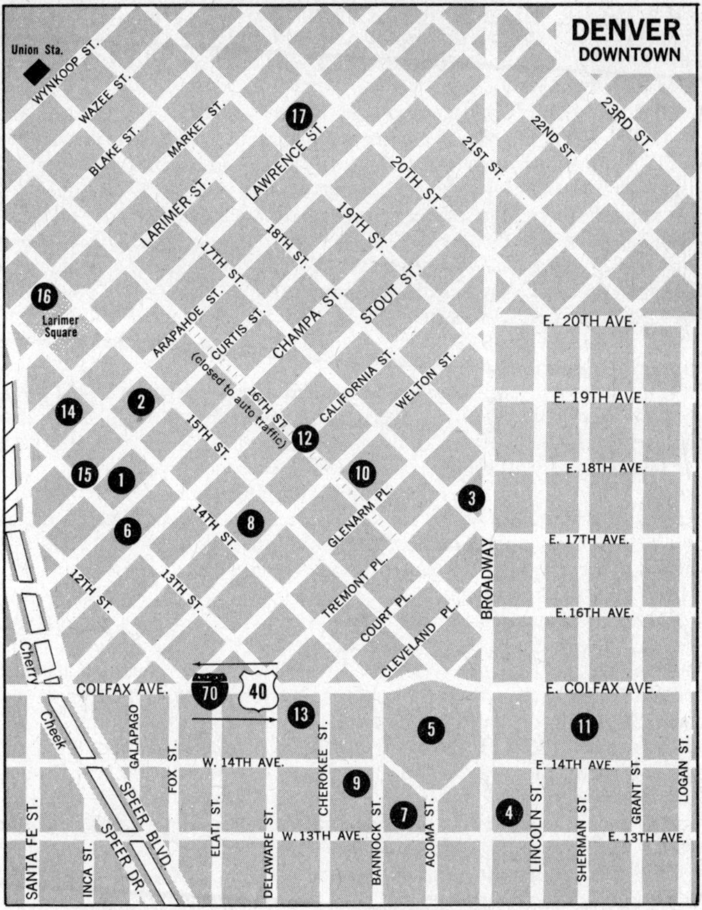

Points of Interest

1) Auditorium Arena & Theater
2) Brooks Tower
3) Brown Palace Hotel
4) Colorado Heritage Center
5) Civic Center
6) Convention Center, Currigan Hall
7) Denver Art Museum
8) Denver Post Building
9) Denver University Law Center
10) Masonic Temple Building
11) State Capitol
12) Sixteenth St. Mall
13) U.S. Mint
14) University of Colorado Administration Building
15) Denver Center for the Performing Arts
16) Larimer Square
17) Sakura Square

(usually until July 5) when it closes for inventory. The second largest cache of gold bullion is on display, too, and souvenir coin sets and other collectors' items may be purchased. Tour hours are 8:30 A.M. to 3 P.M., Monday through Friday.

The Mint stands on the west side of Denver's **Civic Center,** a three-block stretch of lawns and gardens. It's the inner city oasis where office workers and tourists picnic, stroll, or just rest. The Greek-style amphitheater on the Center's south edge was built in 1919 and was once used for concerts, religious services, and public meetings. The curved walkways on each side display the Colonnades of Civic Benefactors, listing in bronze letters the prominent folks who donated for the Center's construction. The area is also rich in statuary.

The Civic Center was inspired by the famous mall in Washington, D.C. and leads visitors to the **Capitol Building** (modeled after the nation's Capitol).

The 160-room building was completed in 1894, with gold leaf hammered from Colorado ore covering the dome. From the balcony just below, visitors can see a 150-mile panorama of the Rockies to the west.

The interior wainscoting is an exotic deep ochre marble found in a single deposit in southern Colorado. Capital construction used the entire deposit; the interior highlights can never be duplicated or replaced. Other interior highlights include murals by famed Colorado artist Allen True, accompanied by verses of Thomas Hornsby Ferril, the state's Poet Laureate.

The 13th step at the entrance marks a point exactly one mile above sea level. Monday through Friday.

Two blocks away at 13th and Broadway is the **Heritage Center,** which houses artifacts and photos from Denver's early life, even ancient Mesa Verde Indian pieces and a fascinating diorama of Denver as it was in 1860. Historic photos are well displayed. Contains the treasures collected by the Colorado Historical Society including many new permanent exhibits. Browse for free, Monday through Friday 9 A.M. to 5 P.M. Opens at 10 A.M. on Saturdays and Sundays; small entrance fee.

The Denver **Public Library** is across Broadway (#1357) from the Heritage Center. Of special interest: the fourth-floor Western History Department. Plenty of information on the old and new West, and Denver in particular, for travelers and history buffs. (James Michener researched some of *Centennial* at these tables.) Open Monday, Tuesday, and Wednesday, 10 A.M. to 9 P.M., closes at 5:30 P.M. Friday and Saturday. Always closed on holidays and Thursdays.

The **Denver Art Museum** towers behind the library. You won't overlook the angular gray-tiled building with windows in seemingly random sizes and shapes. Italian architect Gio Ponti designed the edifice to house the museum's collection in style. The items span cultures as well as time: African, Oriental, pre-Columbian, and early American, with one or two masterpieces by Rembrandt, Picasso, Matisse, Renoir, Rubens, and others, including much contemporary art. There are also textiles, costumes, pottery, jewelry, period rooms, and antique furniture. The Native American exhibit is execllent. Open Tuesday through Saturday, 10 A.M. to 4:30 P.M., Sunday 1 P.M. to 5 P.M. and Wednesday evening; small daily entrance "contribution" and a charge for special exhibits.

At 1340 Pennsylvania Street, just east of the Historical Museum, the **Molly Brown House** has recently been rescued from destruction. This home of the "unsinkable" lady celebrated from Broadway to Hollywood had become a dilapidated boardinghouse until preservationists purchased and restored it.

J.J. and Molly Brown met and married in Leadville, Colorado, in 1886. When J.J.'s gold claim proved to be among the richest ever struck, the Browns moved to Denver. Molly desperately wanted to be part of Denver's high society, which ridiculed her as a "rustic." She traveled extensively in Europe and eventually took her revenge: when friends she made on the Continent—including royalty and famous artists and authors—came calling on her, she didn't invite those same social lions who now courted her.

Molly Brown became a national heroine in 1912 when, returning from a European trip, she took charge of a rescue party as the *Titanic* sank and personally saved several lives. The house has been restored from photographs, with much of the original furniture. Summer tour hours 10 A.M. to 3 P.M.; noon to three during the rest of the year. Tues. to Sat.

Straight south of Molly's place, at 8th Avenue and Pennsylvania, is another famous residence, the **Colorado Governor's Mansion.** It's surrounded by terraced gardens and ancient elms.

Built in 1908 by Walter Cheesman, the twenty-seven-room house was later owned by the John Evanses, then by the Claude Boettcher family who donated it to the state in 1958. The magnificent interiors and lavish furnishings were conceived and assembled through the Boettchers' extensive world travels. The house is open for tours on Tuesdays only; no charge.

Back in the heart of downtown, one block behind the Visitors' Bureau, you'll discover the **Denver Firefighters Museum** at 1326 Tremont Place. Old hand pumpers, uniforms, photos, and other items are housed in Fire House No. 1, built in 1909. Tours 10 A.M. to 4 P.M., closed Mondays. Small entry fee.

A few blocks away at 15th and California streets the *Denver Post* —which became one of the nation's great newspapers—offers daily tours of a working newspaper plant; on the hour from noon to 3 P.M. Nearby **Currigan Exhibition Hall,** 14th & Champa, hosts many shows, conventions, and festivals. **The Buckhorn Exchange,** at 1000 Osage Street, close to downtown, is worth a visit just before lunch-time. Several generations have enriched this museum and dining emporium. Contents include hundreds of historic photos (some of the Tabors, for instance), ancient western guns, trophies and antlers of every description, stuffed animals, Indian mementos, paintings. Free entrance. See also restaurants (American).

The heart of Denver's phenomenal boom is **17th Street,** the city's financial district. Here, amid more than a dozen new office towers of glass, chrome, and steel, many of the *Fortune* 500 companies occupy sleek new offices. The Anaconda Corporation, an international mining and minerals conglomerate, completed a forty-story office tower next to the gleaming Fairmont Hotel.

The nation's leaders in finance, in industry, and in engineering are flocking here to pursue the richest concentration of energy reserves in the nation. As you walk "Seventeenth" you will overhear conversations about new petroleum finds, multi-million-dollar mining projects, new technical advances.

A brief walk west, just across Speer Boulevard, is the new **Auraria Higher Education Center.** Metro State College, Denver Community College, and Colorado University all use the ultra-modern educational village. Don't miss **9th Street Historic Park,** tucked behind the classroom building. It's a block of restored Victorian working-class houses from one of the earliest settlements of Denver, now used as offices for the colleges. The ornate white building with the blue roof at the foot of the campus is the old **Tivoli Brewery,** which operated from 1882 until 1969.

The highlight of downtown Denver sightseeing is **Larimer Square,** on Larimer Street between 14th and 15th. This is the city's original business block. Denver had abandoned lower Larimer Street since the early 1900s, leaving it to vagrants and disrepair until a local preservation group rescued the buildings and restored them to become Denver's first officially designated Historic District. Larimer Square contains all manner of shops and exotica: bistros, fine restaurants, silversmiths and leatherworkers' studios.

Across the Platte River on 15th Street is the **Forney Transportation Museum,** filled with vintage vehicles, "pufferbellies" and historic railroad cars, old-time airplanes, and more. The **Denver Children's Museum** is down the block at 931 Bannock with special "hands on" exhibits and weekend storytellers.

Denver is also the home of the **National Western Stock Show,** an annual January event since 1905. The world's largest single livestock exhibition, this trade show of the ranching industry draws visitors from Canada and Mexico as well as from the entire United States. It is said that millions of dollars in business deals get settled here each year. Events include professional and amateur rodeo, several horse shows, and the judging of champion cattle. All stock show events are held at the Denver Coliseum, I–70 and Washington Street.

Other Points of Interest

The **Denver Botanic Gardens** at 909 York Street offers seasonal displays, herbal acreage, and a two-acre classic Japanese garden. The conservatory, looking like a quilted bubble, shelters an authentic tropical/subtropical forest with streams, paths, foot bridges. Daily, 9 A.M. to 4:45 P.M. Open all year.

City Park, northeast of the Botanic Gardens along 17th Avenue between York Street and Colorado Boulevard, yields 640 acres for recreation and learning. Start at the **Museum of Natural History**—four floors of dinosaurs, Indian artifacts, insects, birds, and animals from around the world. Don't miss the moose and elk displays and the whale exhibit. Headphones that plug into outlets at each display for brief talks can be rented. The **Gates Planetarium,** attached to the museum, offers laser light concerts and trips through time and space projected onto an overhead fifty-foot dome while the audience watches from reclining chairs.

A short walk west takes you to the **Denver Zoo.** More than 1,500 animals are housed in native habitats. The Children's Zoo here sports a monkey island and cavorting seals. There is also a walk-through Bird House. The well-groomed, flowered, and landscaped expanse of City Park is the centerpiece of Denver's 25,000-acre municipal park system.

Elitch Gardens at West 38th Avenue at Tennyson Street is loosely patterned after the Tivoli Gardens in Copenhagen, Denmark. Elitch offers dozens of children's rides. The "Mister Twister" roller coaster climbs to a height of 96 feet, then plummets through two speed spirals and into a winding tunnel. Plenty of refreshments. June through Labor Day, 11 A.M. to 11 P.M. Just north, at Sheridan Boulevard and I–70, there is **Lakeside Amusement Park,** with many more rides, a fun house, penny arcades, and even an auto racetrack.

Red Rocks Park can be found above the small town of Morrison on Denver's far western edge. It takes about thirty minutes to reach Red Rocks from the city's center. Best route: the 6th Avenue Freeway west to Interstate 70; turn south on I–70 and get off at the next exit so you'll be driving south on Hog Back Road toward Morrison. The red sandstone formations, thrust skyward by the ancient upheaval of a prehistoric ocean bed, leave an impact on the first-time viewer. Lots of space for hiking and exploring. Casual climbs on the rocks are not advisable, however.

Everything is giant at the Red Rocks Park, including the natural amphitheater. For years, the theater was used for ballet and classical music performances. The cost was formidable, however, and mountain gusts would carry away the sound. Now, with modern improvements, Red Rocks is the site of well-attended summer pop music, as well as rock concerts. Although expensive, tickets often sell out weeks in advance.

Golden

Golden, Denver's farthest western suburb, spread along the banks of Clear Creek as a pioneer camp in 1859. It became the capital of Colorado Territory in 1862, and still boasts many buildings from pioneer days. According to a banner over the main street, Golden is "Where the West Remains." The internationally respected Colorado School of Mines is located on the west edge of the town.

The **Railroad Museum** at 17155 West 44th Avenue, has an 1880s-style depot, historical exhibits, old narrow-gauge locomotives, railroad and trolley cars. Open 9 A.M. to 5 P.M. daily. Entrance fee.

The **Foothills Art Center,** 15th and Washington, was originally a Presbyterian church built in 1892, and later a Unitarian church. The art center, showing regional arts and crafts daily all year, was opened in 1968.

Colorado School of Mines' **Geologic Museum** is nearby at 16th and Maple. The 1940 structure displays mineral ore, fossils, mining equipment, meteorites, and even a replica of an old gold mine. Open 10 A.M. to 3 P.M. Monday through Friday, 1 P.M. to 4 P.M. Sunday. Closed Saturdays.

Lookout Mountain, above Golden, just west on I–70, holds a grave of Buffalo Bill Cody at the summit. Also a museum displaying relics of his cavalry and Wild West Show days; well-stocked gift shop. No charge. Open every day, 8:30 A.M. to 4:30 P.M.

Hikers and nature worshippers should drive up to the *Jefferson County Conference and Nature Center,* 900 Colorow Road. It offers a small botanical museum, plus trails.

On the way to Lookout Mountain you may wish to leave I–70 and visit the **Mother Cabrini Shrine.** There is no charge to enter the church, devoted to Saint Francis Xavier Cabrini. The setting includes a large number of meadows, summer flowers, surrounding forests and quite a few steps that will make young walkers happy but can cause older ones to puff a little. Free.

Also consider a trip to **Heritage Square,** southeast of town and one mile west on the intersection of US 6 and 40. The rustic artisan and entertainment village has shops with metalsmiths, jewelers, candymakers, and more. There is an alpine slide, a stable for horseback rides, a narrow-gauge train trip, and a large melodrama theater. Tree-lined, lamplighted streets and plenty of free parking. Heritage Square is open every day all year but is busiest in summer. Shops and amusement park keep varied hours.

PRACTICAL INFORMATION FOR DENVER

HOW TO GET AROUND. By bus: the Denver R.T.D. (Regional Transportation District) operates the city's buses. Buses run not only within Denver proper, but also out into the suburbs and to Boulder. Route and schedule information is available by calling 778-6000. Basic city fare: 35¢; 70¢ at peak hours; exact change.

By taxi: cabs in Denver may be hailed or requested by phone. Taxis are usually plentiful in the city. Yellow Cab, 292-1212, is one of the major operators, or call Zone Cab, 861-2323.

From the airport: taxi service to and from the airport is expensive. For individuals, airport limousine service, which stops at the major hotels, costs a modest $5. Call 398-2284.

TOURIST INFORMATION. For information and brochures about Denver contact the Hospitality Center, Denver and Colorado Convention Visitors' Bureau, 225 W. Colfax Ave., Denver 80202, (303) 892-1112.

TOUR OPERATORS. Several services are available for sightseeing. *AA Sightseeing Tours* combines a city trip and a mountain drive of 5 hours, leaving at 8 A.M. or 1 P.M. Their 14-passenger vans will pick you up at your hotel.

Gray Line offers a 2-hour city tour at 9 A.M. and 2 P.M., and a drive to mountain parks at 9 A.M. that lasts 4 hours. Gray Line will combine the city and mountain trips at a discount fare, and offers special trips to Pikes Peak, Central City, and, in summer, Rocky Mountain National Park. Your hotel will contact Gray Line for your pickup. The preservation group, *Historic Denver, Inc.,* arranges tours of "old Denver," June through September. Tel.: 832-7645.

You can stay grounded with *The Mountain Men,* 11100 E. Dartmouth 219, Denver, Colo. 80014, tel.: 750-0090, who conduct half- and full-day mountain excursions in their own comfortable four-wheel-drive vehicles. A picnic lunch is furnished free in summer with the full-day outing.

Many of the smaller cities and towns have *taxi companies* that will gladly take the tourist on a sightseeing trip in the local area. In the fall a number of "*Aspencades*" depart from various towns to view the spectacular colors of the changing leaves. Check with local chambers of commerce for exact dates and times. *Jeep tours* are popular in various parts of the state as a way to enjoy the mountains and get into little-traveled areas in a manner more comfortable than on the back of a horse or by foot. Again, local chambers of commerce can help in arrangements.

A leisurely way to see downtown Denver is with *Historic Denver Van Tours, Inc.,* tel. 832-7645. The two-hour drive covers historic Denver. Also available are *Denver Walking Tours,* tel. 832-7645.

And more for young ones: *Kids Day Get Away Tours,* tel. 756-7897. Certified teachers lead childrens' groups on 6-hour city and mountain outings, June through August, with special evening tours Tuesdays and Thursdays. Reservations a must.

SEASONAL EVENTS. January: *National Western Stock Show and Rodeo* takes place for nine days in mid-month. The *Western Annual Exhibition* at the Denver Art Museum opens and runs into *March.*

February: *Garden and Home Show.*

March: *Denver Symphony Run* (marathon benefit). *St. Patrick's Day Parade* downtown.

April: *Easter Sunrise services* at Red Rocks. *Denver Bears* baseball season opens.

May: *Lakeside Amusement Park,* and *Elitch Gardens, Theatre and Bands* open to run throughout the summer. Thoroughbred and quarter-horse racing at *Centennial Race Track* begins, with pari-mutuel betting through mid-Nov. In May, the *Denver People's Fair* takes place on the East High School grounds.

June: *Greyhound racing* at Mile High Kennel Club throughout the summer, with pari-mutuel betting. Annual cherry blossoms festival on Sakura Square.

July: Free *band concerts* through Aug. in City Park.

August: *Rocky Mountain Bluegrass Festival.*

September: *Denver Broncos* professional football season opens.

October: Early in the month is the *Lorimer Square Oktoberfest.* The *Denver Symphony* and *Bonfils Memorial Theater* begin eight- and nine-month seasons.

December: Lights are turned on for the *Denver Civic Center Christmas Display.* Larimer Square has the yearly *Christmas Walk,* and the Denver Art Museum has the *Colorado Biennial Art Show.*

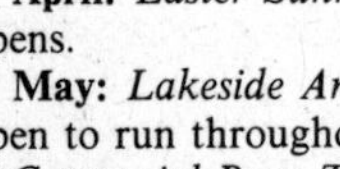

NIGHTLIFE. Denver's teeming nightlife can leave a visitor—even a resident—with many choices. Serious plays, "melodramas," opera, concerts, ballets, choirs, nightclubs, or just "atmosphere" lounges abound.

Some of the city's cultural and entertainment activities now originate from the *Denver Center for the Performing Arts,* downtown between Speer Blvd. and

14th St. and from Champa to Arapahoe Sts. The DCPA is home to both the Denver Symphony, a variety of theater groups, plus a cinema. The Denver Center for the Performing Arts, 14th & Curtis, has tours of *Boettcher Concert Hall* and the *Theater Complex* at noon, Monday through Friday.

The symphony's super-modern *Boettcher Concert Hall* was built at a cost of over $13 million and uses up-to-date accoustic technology. Seating for 2,650 people is arranged around the orchestra on a series of gallery levels and suspended seating rings strategically placed for acoustical excellence. Also, a canopy of 106 "sound discs" distributes the sound to both listeners and performers. The translucent discs are suspended from the ceiling in a spiral nebula. Thirty of these are adjustable so the hall may be "tuned" for different events.

The internationally respected Denver Symphony offers a full season of concerts at the Boettcher Hall from September through May. There are also several free concerts each year. Call the box office in Denver at 292-1584 for schedules and programs, or write 1245 Champa St., 80204.

Area chamber groups and soloists perform throughout the year at the *Arvada Center for the Arts and Humanities,* 6901 Wadsworth Blvd., and the *Houston Fine Arts Center* of Colorado Women's College, Montview Boulevard and Quebec.

Theatergoers will find an equally enticing variety. Across the DCPA Galleria from the Concert Hall is the *Theater Complex,* a $12 million group of four auditoriums. The *Thrust Theater,* also called The *Stage,* holds seating for 660, which may be raised or lowered in five separate sections to create different performing areas. The *Space,* which seats 440, is a theater in the shape of a pentagon and rimmed by a balcony. This allows directors flexibility in the staging of a play. The *Lab* features experimental theater. The Complex is headquarters for Denver's new *Repertory Theater,* opened in 1979 by the former director of the famed Tyrone Guthrie Theater in Minneapolis.

Nearby is the *Auditorium Theater,* for years Denver's only large stage facility. It is still used for productions and for the Broadway shows—with original casts and stars—that regularly come to town. For information on all upcoming DCPA theater events, write to 1053 13th Street, Denver 80202.

The *Elitch Theater,* W. 38th Ave. at Tennyson St., next to the amusement park, is America's oldest summer stock company. The curtain went up on its first performance in 1891. Broadway plays are still performed in the original wooden hall during the summer season. Luminaries who've performed here include Sarah Bernhardt, Grace Kelly, and William Shatner. This well-known attraction is located at 4620 W. 38th Ave., Denver 80212. Reservations needed several weeks in advance. Closed in winter.

The *Bonfils Theater* at 2526 E. Colfax presents good actors from the community, September through June, with several children's shows. The Bonfils' *Bo-Ban's Cabaret* presents mostly Off-Broadway fare. The drama department at the University of Denver presents a selection of plays throughout the year, with interesting and unusual settings.

Denver abounds in small, yet ambitious, professional little theater groups. Among the better ones: The *Changing Scene,* 1527 Champa St.; the previously mentioned *Gaslight Theatre,* 4201 Hooker St.; *Germinal Stage Denver,* 1820 Market St.; *Slightly Off Center Theatre,* 2557 15th St.; the *Comedy Works* offers stand-up comics Wednesdays through Sundays (Larimer Square).

Jazz and Pop: Try *Zeno's Jazz Club* at 5579 S. Windemere. At *Josephina's,* 1433 Larimer, you can enjoy "swinging jazz" in a lusty Italian café. A nice compromise: the San Marco Room of the *Brown Palace Hotel,* Broadway at E. 18th Ave., where an orchestra plays old dance tunes while you dine. Don't miss the jazz concerts at the *Paramount Theater,* 519 16th St., downtown. Every six or eight weeks, local jazz buffs bring in national talent for a jam.

Rock and disco: The scene centers in Glendale, a nearby suburb that has now been completely surrounded by Denver expansion. Leetsdale Dr. east from Colorado Blvd. is the main area for action; the places to try include *Confetti's,* 350 S. Birch, and *Chaps Saloon,* 5231 Leetsdale. *Mr. Lucky's* at 555 S. Cherry is a rock-and-roll roadhouse for the younger crowd. The *Mercury Cafe,* 1308 Pearl, features an exciting spectrum of music by local and out-of-town bands. Big-name rockers appear regularly at the *Rainbow Music Hall,* 6360 E. Evans Ave. and in the summer at *Red Rocks* and *McNichols Arena.*

Revues: Try *The Turn of the Century* at 7300 E. Hampden, southeast. The Turn has an intimate nightclub where national top names give their best, just as they do in Las Vegas or Lake Tahoe.

Folk and Country: Muddy Waters of the Platte Coffee House, just north of downtown at 2557 15th St., serves up guitarists who play for tips, great pastries, and a flock of local "characters." The *Swallow Hill Music Assn.* hosts accoustic concerts at various locations (778-8711).

SHOPPING. Downtown, retail shops line the 16th St. Mall from Court Pl. to Arapahoe St. Here you will find most major department stores: *May D&F* (D&F stands for Daniels & Fisher, a local firm that merged with the May Company years ago), the *Denver Dry Goods Company* and *J. C. Penney.* Don't ignore the smaller shops: *Grassfield's* (for fashions) at 16th and Stout and *Homer Reed* at 1717 Tremont Pl. are tops for men's fashions. (16th St. has been closed to motorized traffic while a grass-and-tree-lined pedestrian mall is being built. The absence of cars makes shopping even more pleasant.)

For newly popular western wear, *Miller Stockman,* 1336 Stout, and *Fred Mueller,* 1409 15th St., carry full arrays of authentic cowboy garb. *Kohlberg's* at 1720 Champa is the best place in the city to find Indian crafts. The store was opened in 1888 and still has its own Indian silversmith; the Kohlbergs are authorities on Pueblo pottery, turquoise, and all Native American arts. You can lose yourself browsing among the rugs, bracelets, and other items.

A short block away, 15th St. also rewards shoppers. *Jerry's News,* 1647 Court, has a good stock of magazines and out-of-town newspapers. *Robert Waxman Camera,* 913 15th St., is a stop for discount cameras, photo supplies and advice.

The Shirt Broker at 1421 Larimer makes shirts and ties to order. *The Market,* 1445 Larimer, offers coffees, pastries, and gourmet delicacies. Near Larimer Square is *Cook Sporting Goods,* among the largest such stores in America. Its rival: *Gart Brothers* at 1000 Broadway, where the "Sports Castle" displays four floors full of gear, including a complete camera department.

For the mountaineer, *Forrest Mountain Shop* at 1517 Platte—north of downtown by the Platte River—offers a full range of rock-climbing supplies, and information on climbing techniques, classes, and groups. *Holubar Mountaineering* at 2490 S. Colorado Blvd. appeals to backpackers.

Before leaving downtown, stop by *Sakura Square* at 19th and Lawrence. You can browse among Oriental grocery, gift, and jade shops in a modern square-block complex.

For more traditional tastes, there is *Cinderella City,* a large shopping mall. A top assortment of clothing, department, and specialty stores. Follow Broadway south of Denver into Englewood, then turn west on Hampden Avenue for eight blocks.

A unique diversion: the *Cherry Creek* shopping area on East 2nd and E. 3rd Aves. between University Blvd. and Cook Sts. Here a concentration of exclusive shops offer brass beds and designer furnishings, *haute couture,* art, and bookshops such as the *Tattered Cover.* The *Aspen Leaf,* 222 Detroit St., supplies sports gear and fashions to the country-club set.

PARKS. Over 150 parks attract city dwellers in droves on the weekends; best time to go is on weekdays, particularly mornings. Most of the parks—especially *City Park*—have show-quality flower gardens, pools, picnic areas, and plenty of trees.

A weekday may be the best day to stroll through Denver's *Washington Park,* at S. Downing and E. Virginia, not far from E. Alameda Ave. These acres of greenery arc almost unknown to tourists, in spite of the attractions: small creeks flow under the branches of willows and cottonwoods. Young lovers from nearby Denver University rendezvous along the trails; elderly gentlemen enjoy a game of *boccie;* a soccer match draws crowds of cheering onlookers; an energetic exercise class comes jogging past. Bring a lunch basket. People walk their dogs, of course, and children sway on swings.

On the drive from downtown to the mountains, consider the greenery surrounding *Sloan's Lake Park* at W. 26th and Sheridan (or reach it from W. Colfax Ave.). On a clear day, the view of the mountain is spectacular from here. Denverites take advantage of this lake for water skiing, sailing, motor boating (no swimming), fishing, bicycling, tennis (courts on both sides), or just walking around. The circle tour takes about one hour on foot.

Actually, Denver's municipal parks stimulate plenty of outdoor life on 2,800 acres; to these, you may add another city-owned 14,000 acres in the foothills.

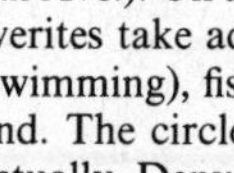

SPECTATOR SPORTS. Denver's area **auto racetracks** offer everything from Indianapolis-type formula cars to motorcycle competition. Nearest is *Lakeside Speedway* at the amusement park, W. 44th Ave. and Sheridan. The Sunday night programs run from early May through Labor Day, with special "demolition derbies" on holidays. Similar events at *Continental Divide Raceway* (south of Denver on I–25 past the town of Castle Rock); *Colorado National Speedway* (north on I–25 to Erie exit #232); and *Englewood Speedway* (2865 West Oxford).

Mile High Stadium, just west of Downtown, is home turf for the Denver Bears **baseball** team. The stadium seats 50,000. The season begins in early April and usually includes almost 70 home games. Next to the stadium, the Denver Nuggets **basketball** team is based in *McNichols Arena.*

Those 74,000 seats in *Mile High Stadium* are never enough to hold all the fans of the Denver Broncos **football** team. The team has improved greatly in recent years and is now a citywide passion. Games frequently sell out in advance.

The Rockies **hockey** team also uses *McNichols Arena* near Mile High Stadium. These tough skaters always put on a good show.

Back downtown, the Denver Comets professional **volleyball** team provides a lively summer schedule at the *Auditorium Arena,* 13th and Champa, usually May through August.

If you have never seen a **dog race,** try the *Mile High Kennel Club* at Colorado Blvd. and East 62nd Ave. The greyhounds run five nights a week, June through August, with matinees on Saturdays. Betting is legal for persons 18 or over. In the winter, the action switches to the *Interstate Kennel Club* in the town of Byers, a half hour east of Denver. Programs every evening but Sunday, with a Saturday matinee as well, from late November to March.

Horse racing takes place at the *Centennial Turf Club,* 5300 S. Federal Blvd. From May through Labor Day, some of the West's best horses and jockeys compete while the audience bets quinellas, daily doubles, and so on. Post times and dates vary. Thoroughbreds race from May through September.

SPORTS. Boating is popular at *Cherry Creek Reservoir,* just southeast of the intersection of Hampden and Havana. The reservoir is crowded on hot weekends. *Sloan's Lake,* at 17th and Sheridan, is for sailors and waterskiers.

The **golf** season lasts virtually for 12 months in Denver. Among the array of courses, consider the scenic *Wellshire Municipal Golf Course,* 3333 S. Colorado Blvd. at Hampden Ave. Eighteen holes, lush grounds, rental equipment, a good restaurant and lounge.

Other golf Links? *City Park,* E. 25th Ave. and York St., and *Park Hill* at 3500 Colorado Blvd., both northeast; *Willis Case,* W. 50th Ave. at Vrain, northwest; the *John Kennedy* course at 10500 E. Hampden Ave., southeast; and *Overland Park,* southwest at West Jewell Avenue at S. Santa Fe Dr. If you belong to a golf or country club back home, you may be extended playing privileges at Denver's private courses. Some of the better ones are *Cherry Hills,* 4000 S. University Blvd.; *Heather Ridge,* 13521 E. Iliff Ave.; and *Pinehurst,* 6255 W. Quincy Ave.

Tennis thrives on free city-maintained courts in most parks, including *Berkeley,* W. 46th Ave. at Tennyson; *Washington Park,* Louisiana at Downing; *Eisenhower,* S. Colorado Blvd. at Dartmouth; *Crestmoor,* E. 1st Ave. at Monaco; and City Park. A little-known spot: *Houston Lake Park,* W. Kentucky Ave. at S. Vallejo St., with four courts beside a lake.

If your hotel or motel doesn't have a **swimming pool,** an Olympic-sized one exists indoors at *Celebrity Sports Center,* 888 S. Colorado Blvd. Steam rooms are offered too.

WHAT TO DO WITH THE CHILDREN. A full day may easily be spent in *City Park,* with its zoo, children's zoo, and playgrounds. The *Denver Museum of Natural History and Planetarium* are in the park and should not be missed. Band concerts are given nightly in the summer months. *Congress Park* has a large outdoor swimming pool. *Elitch Gardens* has a delightful kiddieland, as well as the usual amusement-park attractions and beautiful flower gardens. *Lakeside Amusement Park,* with stock-car races, speedboating, and amusement rides, has long been a favorite with the young. *Celebrity Sports Center* features game arcades and bowling. The *Denver Public Library* and *Phipps Auditorium* often have films or lectures of interest to children. Both boys and girls will enjoy the *Wax Museum* or the *Forney Transportation Museum.* The *Children's Museum* offers special exhibits plus live weekend story tellers. *Miniature golf* in the summer will keep youngsters busy at *Zeckendorf Plaza* at May-D&F. The *Colorado Railroad Museum,* in a depot-style building, houses many early Colorado railroad items. A trip to *The Fort,* an authentic reproduction of Bent's Fort, may be of interest—your children may eat a piece of buffalo meat and browse in the trading post. From June to August, *Kids Get Away Tours* offers children ages 6–12 a Denver or mountain tour. The fee includes all expenses, even meals and transportation.

HOTELS AND MOTELS in Denver range from the old, established, world-famous Brown Palace through its sister lodgings in the deluxe and expensive categories, then on to the many fine hotels scattered along the metropolitan area's highways and side streets. Many of the latter are connected to national chain operations. Cost figures are generally for the minimum or moderate-priced rooms, unless a range is indicated. Listings are in order of price category.

The price categories in this section, for double occupancy, will average as follows: *Deluxe* \$55–\$100, *Expensive* \$35–\$54, *Moderate* \$21–\$34, and *Inexpensive* \$14–\$20. For a more complete description of these categories, see the *Hotels and Motels* part of *Facts at Your Fingertips* at the front of this volume.

Brown Palace. *Deluxe.* Tremont and 17th Sts. One of the world's well-known hotels, good service, 500 guest rooms, and tasteful decoration. Elegant dining in the "Palace Arms" or the "San Marco Room," relaxed meals in the "Ship Tavern," where prime rib reigns. Beauty and barber shops, florist, drugstore.

Denver Granada Royale. *Deluxe.* 7525 East Hampden. Suites. Meeting and seminar facilities. Indoor pool. Shopping nearby.

Denver Hilton. *Deluxe.* 1550 Court Pl. A large establishment catering to Colorado's major conventions. The block-long second floor lobby is unusual. Five dining areas and handsome cocktail lounge. Heated pools, saunas, color TV, radios, barber and beauty shops, drugstore, airport bus available. Underground parking. Upper stories yield view of the Rockies.

Denver Marriott City Center. *Deluxe.* 1701 California. New 42-story 612-room hotel. 42 luxury suites. Indoor pool. Ballrooms. Restaurants and bars. In downtown financial center. Ideal for conventions.

Denver Marriott Hotel. *Deluxe.* I–25 at Hampden. Excellent location en route to Colorado Springs. All the modern facilities/amenities. 605 quality rooms. Convention facilities. Indoor-outdoor pool. Restaurants. Recommended.

Executive Tower. *Deluxe.* 1405 Curtis St. Downtown skyscraper hotel, popular with convention guests. Health and athletic club. Ballroom. Restaurants.

Fairmont Hotel. *Deluxe.* 1750 Welton. Denver's elegant $44 million 550-room convention hotel. All amenities. Marquis dining room. Twenty-four-hour McGuire's deluxe coffee shop. Rooftop pool, "Sky court" tennis.

Hampshire House Hotel. *Deluxe.* 1000 Grant St. Distinguished small hotel close to downtown and state capital. Kitchens. Some suites and kitchenettes. Favored by upper echelon business executives.

Regency Inn. *Deluxe.* 3900 Elati St., I–25 at W. 38th Ave. A large hotel in north Denver, popular with conventions. Two pools, saunas, exercise rooms, barber and beauty shops, gourmet restaurant and cocktail lounge.

Sheraton Denver Tech Center. *Deluxe.* At Tech Center, 12 mi. southeast of downtown Denver. Built in 1980. 327 rooms, plus conference and banquet facilities and shops.

Stapleton Plaza. *Deluxe.* 3333 Quebec. "A touch of glass." Atrium, skylight and other architectural innovations. Elegant guest rooms and suites. Athletic center.

Stouffer's Denver Inn. *Deluxe.* 3203 Quebec. At airport. A well-run, 588-room super motel with large indoor pool, sauna, and outstanding dining facilities. Complimentary airport limousine.

Writers Manor. *Deluxe.* 1730 S. Colorado Blvd. A large, 350-room spacious motel with two heated pools, sauna. Churchill Gourmet Restaurant, coffee shops, and bars.

Plaza Suites. *Expensive to Deluxe.* 4550 East Jewell. Apartment hotel for nightly guests. Maid service. Pool. Color Tv. Free airport limousine.

Ramada Renaissance. *Expensive to Deluxe.* I–225 and S. Parker Rd. Relatively new hostelry with all amenities, including an indoor jogging track. Large convention area with ballroom.

Rodeway Inn. *Expensive to Deluxe.* 4590 Quebec. Five minutes from Stapleton Airport, courtesy car. Special rooms offer private steambath, recliner chairs, office-size work desks. Bijou Revue restaurant and lounge. Entertainment.

Airport Hilton Inn. *Expensive.* Peoria and I–70. Good location near airport. Restaurant.

Best Western Inn at the Mart. *Expensive.* I–25, Exit 215. Popular with sales reps. Shops, cafés, post office on premises. Convention site.

Governor's Court Hotel. *Expensive.* Grant and 17th. Formerly the Radisson.

Holiday Inn Downtown. *Expensive.* 15th and Glenarm. 400-room hotel in excellent location. Free indoor parking.

Holiday Inn Southeast. *Expensive.* At Denver Tech Center, I–25. Suites available. Indoor pool, sauna, exercise room, steam room. Live entertainment and dancing nightly except Sunday and Monday. Dining room, cocktail lounge and coffee shop. Good location, south.

Howard Johnson's Motor Lodge South. *Expensive.* Exit 201, I–25 (south). Modern chain motel. Restaurant, cocktail lounge, guest laundry, meeting and banquet facilities.

Ramada Inn. *Expensive.* Good location at 1150 E. Colfax and Downing. 150 rooms, nicely redecorated. Popular with sales people. Small outdoor courtyard pool. Bar and restaurant.

Ramada Inn Foothills. *Expensive.* 6th Ave. and Simms, on the way to the ski areas. Pool and sauna. Attractive establishment. Elegant lobby. Plush rooms.

Rodeway Inn, Airport. *Expensive.* 4590 Quebec. Rooms offer TV. Meeting facilities. Free shuttle to airport. Restaurants.

Sheraton Denver, Airport. *Expensive.* 3535 Quebec St. at Stapleton Airport. This modern hotel offers indoor heated pool, sauna, health club, restaurant and cocktail lounge. Free airport bus.

Broadway Plaza. *Moderate.* Broadway at 11th Ave., 4 blks. south of State Capitol. In addition to 40 clean rooms, there are rooftop sun deck, free coffee. Privately owned motel. Cafés nearby.

Colburn Hotel. *Moderate.* 980 Grant Street, close to downtown area. All rooms with baths. Some kitchenettes and facilities for permanent guests. Charlie Brown's Dining Room plus cocktail lounge.

Denver Central TraveLodge. *Moderate.* Valley Hwy,. at Speer Blvd. Small motel offers free coffee, sun deck. 24-hour coffee shop nearby.

Eddie Bohn's Pig N' Whistle. *Moderate.* 4801 W. Colfax. Well-known old motel with steakhouse.

Kipling Inn. *Moderate.* 715 Kipling St., 9½ mi. southwest just off US 6 in Lakewood. This west Denver motel offers heated pool, playground, restaurant, and cocktail lounge. Some units with kitchens.

La Quinta. *Moderate.* 3975 Peoria, not far from airport. Newish chain motel. 112 rooms. Denny's café.

Quality Inn Downtown. *Moderate.* Valley Hwy, at N. Speer Blvd. This large, easily accessible motel offers a large heated pool, free coffee, dining room, coffee shop, cocktail lounge, dancing. Recently refurbished.

Quality Inn Four Winds. *Moderate.* 4600 W. Colfax. Near Sloan's Lake, en route to mountains.

Sands Motel. *Moderate.* 13388 E. Colfax. Waterbeds available. Some kitchens.

Spa Motor Inn. *Moderate.* On I–25, 8th Ave. exit. Basic motor hotel on Denver's busiest highway; near downtown. Cafe and bar.

American Family Lodge. *Inexpensive.* 5888 N. Broadway, 4 mi. north at I–25 exit 110. Good family motel. Large, attractive rooms, heated pool, playground.

American Family Lodge-West. *Inexpensive.* 4735 Kipling St., 8 mi. west on I–70 on Wheatridge (exit #65). Heated pool. 24-hour cafe opposite.

Anchor. *Inexpensive.* 2323 S. Broadway, 4 mi. south on State 87. Small motel, free coffee, pets, sun deck. 24-hour cafe nearby. Good value.

Motel Six. *Inexpensive.* Wadsworth at I–25 (west). Bargain rates for simple, nondescript rooms. Clean. Fills up early in the day. En route to mountains.

Motel Six. *Inexpensive.* Peoria and I–70 (east). Basic accommodations in chain motel. Popular with budgeteers.

Regal 8. *Inexpensive.* I–70 and Peoria. Chain motel.

Rosedale Motel. *Inexpensive.* 3901 Elati, off I–25 at 38th Ave. A modest motel with clean rooms. Credit cards accepted.

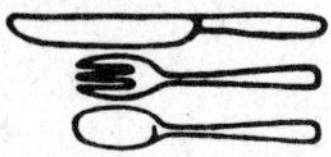

DINING OUT. The restaurants of Denver and its large metropolitan area are often underestimated. There are approximately 1,700 restaurants, cafés, bistros, pizza places, franchises, taverns serving food, cafeterias, and other establishments where you can eat. You can find every type of fare in Denver—from *haute cuisine* to the simplest cowboy fare. Foreign restaurants proliferate, Western steak houses are abundant, and practically everywhere, you can get excellent mountain trout.

While many excellent restaurants go in for international cuisine, those serving steak and lobster are prevalent and popular. Most good restaurants prefer that reservations be made for dinner. At most places, dress is casual; ties are rarely required, for instance. Prices are for the medium-priced meals unless a range is indicated. For other worthwhile restaurants, check hotel listings. Restaurants are listed in order of price category.

Restaurant categories are: *Deluxe* $21 and up, *Expensive* $10–$20, *Moderate* $6–$9, and *Inexpensive* $3–$6. These prices are for appetizer, salad or soup, plus entrée, exclusive of drinks and tips.

Rating restaurants is, at best, a subjective business, and naturally a matter of personal taste. It is, therefore, difficult to call a restaurant "the best" and hope to get unanimous agreement. The following are our choices of the best eating places in Denver.

American and Western

Wuthering Heights. *Deluxe.* 7785 E. Colfax, block west of Wadsworth on west side. Old World atmosphere created by armored knights, red lamps, fireplaces, pewter. American menu. Combinations available: lobster and prime rib; crab legs and steaks. Selection of 20 entrées, and good house wines. Recommended despite lack of adequate lighting.

Coach House. *Expensive to Deluxe.* 10607 Dartmouth. One of the area's most reliable restaurants for quantities of quality food. Free appetizer Lazy Susan. Delicious romaine salad. Tender tournedos and other meats. Fresh fish. Manager James Kallas always on hand. Nourishing desserts. A well-run restaurant.

Bobby McGee's. *Expensive.* 10175 E. Hampden. Theme restaurant with staff dressed as comic characters and TV personalities. Remarkably good service and solid Western food. Loud disco music attracts young crowd.

Buckhorn Exchange. *Expensive.* 1000 Osage St. A Denver institution since 1893 (see also *Museums*). Friendly, informal, truly Western eatery near downtown. Famous bean soup. Steaks of several sizes, buffalo meat, quail, and trout. Nightly specials. Cordial bar. Hundreds of pictures, animal heads, stuffed creatures for decoration. Busy. Excellent value.

Eugene's. *Expensive.* 235 Fillmore St., in Cherry Creek Shopping area. You dine in a courtyard among planters, or in the paneled deluxe restaurant itself, under subdued lights. Drinks are as generous as the portions of veal Zürich, beef Wellington, steak Diane, Dover sole, and other fare; good service. Imported wines. Swiss management.

Palace Arms. *Expensive.* Brown Palace Hotel. This is the choice of Denver's Old Guard, and favorite with business executives. Known for native steaks. If the Palace Arms is full, ask for the San Marco Room. Both also cater to the luncheon crowd. Ties essential at Palace Arms.

Summerfields. *Expensive.* At Ramada Renaissance, S. Parker Rd. Large number of well-cooked entrées. Fish buffet every Friday. Outstanding Sunday brunch. Excellent management.

Victoria Station. *Expensive.* 4330 E. Alameda. Railroad-inspired restaurant features darkish railroad cars, cabooses, old lanterns. Passengers patronize salad bar, and go for a repast of mostly meats: various steaks, London broils, top sirloins, "engine men's cuts" of prime ribs.

Cork'n Cleaver. *Moderate to Expensive.* 4042 E. Virginia, near Colorado Blvd. Menu on a hatchet features mostly beef dishes. Nice salad bar, cocktails, pretty waitresses. Fireplaces light up the darkness for a mostly 20–35 age crowd. Pleasant dining experience.

Apple Tree Shanty. *Moderate.* 8710 E. Colfax. Takes no reservations but usually enough room for families. Pit-prepared ribs a house specialty. Sizable dessert menu. Waitresses in Dutch-style garb.

North Woods Inn. *Moderate.* 6115 S. Santa Fe Dr., 12 mi. southwest on US 85 in Littleton. This locally popular restaurant serves steak, beef stew, and logging-camp food with homebaked sourdough bread. The décor is north woods. Good value for big eaters.

White Fence Farm. *Moderate to Inexpensive.* 6263 W. Jewell Ave. between S. Sheridan and Wadsworth Blvds. In a meadow en route to mountains. (Car needed.) Great American food with a southern accent—ham, turkey, chicken, ribs, prepared Colonial style and served by girls in historic dress. Freshly baked goods. Liquor. Excellent quality food. Mostly local clientele. Dinner only.

Magic Pan. *Inexpensive.* Handsome pancake house on Larimer Sq., 1464 Larimer St. Brightly furnished, well-lighted, always pleasant restaurant. Stews, crêpes, pancakes, desserts. Liquor license. Reliable quality. Separate area for smokers.

British/Irish

Bull & Bush. *Expensive.* Dexter and S. Cherry Creek Dr. Congenial, noisy English pub for ages 25–35.

Oak Room. *Expensive.* 3203 Quebec at Stouffer's Denver Inn. Warm manor atmosphere, with many appetizers and excellent entrées. Menu tucked inside an English encyclopedia, soft classical music and other Olde Worlde touches.

French and Continental

Churchill's. *Deluxe.* At Writer's Manor, 1730 S. Colorado Blvd. Candle lit and cosmopolitan. Fresh fish daily. Fine veal. Experienced European chef makes this one of Denver's gourmet outposts.

Marquis. *Deluxe.* French and Continental. At the Fairmont Hotel, 1750 Welton St. (downtown). Contemporary décor of glass and chrome; lighted ice carvings, elegant tableside cooking. French menu includes avocados and lobster for hors d'oeuvre, French goose liver with truffles (at $33), oysters Rockefeller. Entrées to match. A triumph to the end, with a lighted pastry cart and silver finger bowls. Late service.

Mon Petit. *Deluxe.* 7000 W. 38th Ave., Wheat Ridge, on the west side, close to the foothills. Dressy. A dining adventure that might be called "Mon Grand." Palatial villa supping. One of the area's most elaborate menu and wine lists. Classy décor, superb service. Muted elegance. A deluxe dining experience. Owner Frank Pourdad always on premises to supervise tuxedoed staff.

Tante Louise. *Deluxe.* Continental. 4900 E. Colfax in East Denver. European-style restaurant; steak au poivre, Canadian hare, veal medallions, fresh flounder and snapper, and lamb shanks. Splendid appetizers, desserts, house wines. Intimate setting. Corbin Douglass III, the suave, long-time manager, knows his clientele.

Antares. *Deluxe to Expensive.* At Stapleton Plaza, 3333 Quebec. Wild boar, tournedos "Helder," medallions of veal Hongroises, flambés, fresh berries in season.

Normandy Restaurant Français. *Deluxe to Expensive.* French. At E. Colfax and Madison. A quiet, cozy, smoothly run restaurant with a long reputation among local gourmets. Interesting appetizers such as smoked trout, Mousseline Neptune, French pâté; excellent veal entrées, coq au beaujolais. Fresh fish daily. A perfect individual beef Wellington; goose at Christmas. Wine cellar with some 250 vintages, including rare imports. Several private rooms. One of the best in Denver. Under 25-year ownership-supervision of M. and Mme. Gerstlé.

Quorum. *Expensive.* Continental. 233 E. Colfax Ave. A classy favorite with politicos. Across from State Capitol. Features smoked trout, steak Diane, veal Oscar, entrecôte au poivre, Dover sole, veal Pyreneés. Flaming desserts. Excellent wine cellar. Multi-lingual owner-chef Pierre Wolfe always on hand. Excellent choice for visitors from Europe. Open for lunch.

Stouffer's Top of the Rockies. *Expensive.* Continental and American. 1616 Glenarm Pl., in the Security Life Bldg., downtown. Swift rides in a glass-enclosed elevator leads you 30 stores above downtown to a good view of the Rockies. Specialties are Chateaubriand, flaming dishes, escargots, marinated mushrooms, mussels remoulade, crabmeat cooked in Chablis. Dancing, entertainment. Good place for lunch, too.

Le Central. *Inexpensive.* 112 E. 8th Ave. Genuine French restaurant at bargain prices. Lunch and dinner. Extremely busy. Many entrées, all excellent. French wines. No credit cards. Near downtown.

German

Gasthaus Ridgeview. *Moderate.* W. 44th at Garrison, in Wheat Ridge. Genuine German offerings for a hungry clientele. Sauerbraten, schnitzel, Kassler, Rindsrouladen, milkfed veal dishes, goose (in December), strudel. Peter Hellerman, proprietor and chef, is from Germany; hostess Elizabeth Hellerman is from Switzerland. Imported beers. Outdoor area for lunch.

Italian and Mexican

Josephinas. *Expensive.* 1433 Larimer. Roaring Twenties ambiance on Larimer Square. Excellent lasagna, spaghetti, pizza, chicken. Bar. Historic building.

The Chili Pepper. *Moderate to Inexpensive.* 21st and Bryant, overlooking downtown Denver. Nice setting. Great Mexican food.

La Fontanella. *Moderate to Inexpensive.* 1700 E. Evans. Popular Italian ristorante for lunch and dinner. Young clientele. Large menu.

Garcia's of Scottsdale. *Moderate to Inexpensive.* 1697 S. Havana, near Buckingham Square. Newish Mexican contemporary entry. All the South of the Border favorites. Mexican background music.

Just Harry's. *Moderate to Inexpensive.* 6th Ave. and Sheridan. Mexican stuffed snapper, chimichangas, flautas, hot guacamole. Large portions. Cozy bar.

Casa Bonita. *Inexpensive.* West Colfax at JCRS Center. Mexican food in a multi-tiered restaurant decorated with murals. Busy and entertaining. Mariachi music. Good for kids. "Mexican" restaurant for Americans.

Old Spaghetti Factory. *Inexpensive.* 1215 18th Ave. Downtown. Pasta served in the old Denver Cable Car Company. Lively and crowded. A great value.

Moroccan

Mataam Fez. *Deluxe.* 4609 E. Colfax. Denver's only Moroccan restaurant. Genuine cous cous, lamb dishes, pastella. Dim lights, heavy pillows. Good Moroccan wines. Reserve several hours for your complete supper.

Oriental

Chiling Restaurant. *Moderate.* 2980 S. Colorado Blvd. Mandarin specialties include unique Mongolian barbecue. Six meats and many sauces, buffet style. Seconds allowed. Interesting Oriental liquor.

Trader Vic's. *Expensive.* 1550 Court Pl., in the Hilton Hotel. Polynesian, Cantonese dishes are served in a bright, South Seas décor. Rumakis, crab Rangoon, curries, barbecued fish, veal, lobster thermidor, mahi mahi among selections. Exotic drinks from the bar. Flaming pupus.

Wellshire Inn. *Expensive.* 3333 S. Colorado Blvd. Elaborate international-Polynesian menu served against a Baronial manor backdrop. Overlooks golf course. Lunch and dinner. Specialties include rack of lamb, spinach salad, fresh fish, vegetarian vegetables, chowchow, chicken with almonds. Teriyaki dishes, Cantonese duck, elegant desserts. The magician here is long-time Denver restaurant man Leo Goto. Outdoor service in summer. Well worth the drive.

Dragon Palace. *Expensive to Moderate.* At Denver Tech Center (Belleview exit). Mandarin and Szechuan restaurant. Imagination, a flair for showmanship, vast choices (10 soups, for instance) and constantly interesting cuisine characterize this comparative newcomer. Delicate Peking duck in pancake dough, abalone with sliced chicken, beef with bamboo shoots and black mushrooms are good choices.

Gasho. *Expensive.* I–25 and E. Bellview. Dramatic tableside hibachi cooking. Good beef, chicken, sole. Popular with tourists. Sake or plum wine available.

Yuan Mongolian Barbeque. *Moderate.* 7555 E. Arapahoe Rd. Mandarin, Cantonese, or Szechuan dishes, plus a Mongolian help-yourself barbecue. Brought to Denver by Yuan Hsin, who still operates the restaurant.

Cathay's. *Inexpensive.* 20th and Market Sts., downtown. Modest Chinese restaurant for budget-conscious diners. Wonton soup, chop suey, chow mein, almond duck. No liquor license.

Lotus Room. *Inexpensive.* W. 9th and Speer. Busy family restaurant, frequented by many Denverites. Excellent chop suey, Chinese duck, and countless other dishes. Good value. Informal.

Seafood

Cafe Kandahar. *Deluxe to Expensive.* 2709 W. Main, Littleton. Outstanding new restaurant housed in former library. Superb, fresh salmon steak, Dover sole estragon, shrimp Dijon; also duck, venison. Decor includes ski relics, photos, posters. Run by well-known Denver restaurateur Richard Williams and ski personality Steve Knowlton.

Boston Half Shell. *Expensive.* 15th at Arapahoe in Brooks Towers. New England harborside décor. Fresh seafood flown in daily. Live Maine lobster is a specialty. Also good salmon, sole, trout. Nightly music in the piano bar.

Cafeterias

Furr's. *Inexpensive.* 700 S. Colorado Blvd. Indoor parking. Clean, modern.

Wyatt's. *Inexpensive.* Villa Italia. Nice shopping center setting. Good food. Special nonsmoking room.

Wyatt's. *Inexpensive.* Two locations: 2910 E. 1st Ave., Cherry Creek Center and 7200 W. Alameda. Excellent value, good atmosphere. Separate area for smokers.

BEYOND DENVER

You have already reached the Mile High City's edges and visited Golden and Morrison. How about venturing farther afield into Colora-

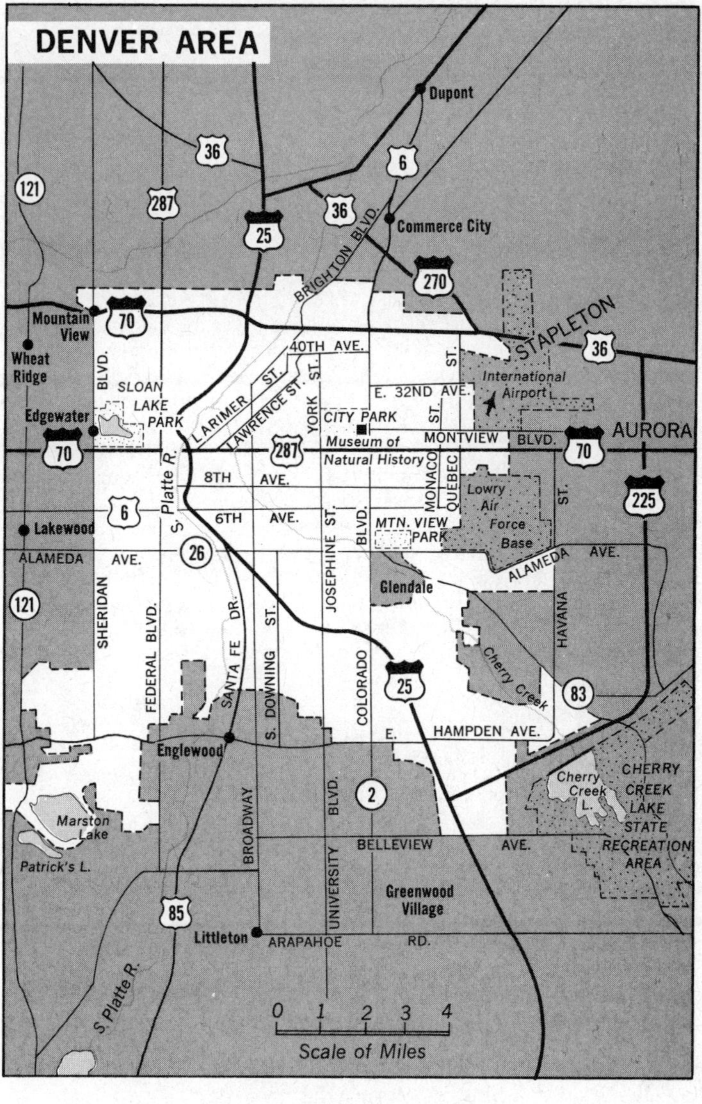
DENVER AREA
Dupont
Commerce City
Mountain View
Wheat Ridge
Edgewater
Lakewood
SLOAN LAKE PARK
STAPLETON International Airport
AURORA
CITY PARK
Museum of Natural History
Lowry Air Force Base
MTN. VIEW PARK
Glendale
Englewood
Marston Lake
Patrick's L.
Cherry Creek
Cherry Creek L.
CHERRY CREEK LAKE STATE RECREATION AREA
Greenwood Village
Littleton
S. Platte R.
BRIGHTON BLVD.
40TH AVE.
LARIMER ST.
LAWRENCE ST.
YORK ST.
E. 32ND AVE.
MONTVIEW BLVD.
8TH AVE.
6TH AVE.
ALAMEDA AVE.
SHERIDAN BLVD.
FEDERAL BLVD.
SANTA FE DR.
S. DOWNING ST.
JOSEPHINE ST.
COLORADO BLVD.
MONACO ST.
QUEBEC ST.
HAVANA ST.
E. HAMPDEN AVE.
BROADWAY
UNIVERSITY BLVD.
BELLEVIEW AVE.
ARAPAHOE RD.
0 1 2 3 4
Scale of Miles

do? Here are some suggestions, all within an approximate fifty-mile radius.

Boulder

Boulder is a half-hour's highway drive north of Denver on US 36 from I–25. As you approach, you'll see the much-photographed reddish sandstone formations known as the "Flatirons," the abrupt border between the plains and the Rocky Mountains. The Flatirons are also a gateway to webs of popular hiking trails in the hills that rise behind the college town. And rock climbers favor these same rocks.

Boulder's tree-lined campus is worth visiting, especially in summer when the University of Colorado stages its yearly **Colorado Shakespeare Festival.** Several Shakespeare plays are performed here in repertory from mid-July through mid-August. Actors are chosen from national auditions. For details, write the Colorado Shakespeare Festival, University of Colorado, Campus Box 261, Boulder, Colo. 80309.

Mid-June through July sees the **Colorado Music Festival** in Boulder, too. Visiting performers and composers lend their talent and energy to the Festival. You will need reservations. Write to the Festival at 1245 Pearl, Boulder, Colo. 80302, for details.

Boulder is headquarters for the **National Center for Atmospheric Research.** Perched on a mesa southwest of town at 1850 Table Mesa Dr., the futuristic complex sits in a nature preserve open to hikers and picnickers. NCAR offers exhibits and afternoon guided tours. The respected *National Bureau of Standards* is also located in this university town.

Evergreen

Evergreen, "the Blue Spruce Capital of the World," was settled in 1859 as a lumber and supply center for the local mining camps. Today, it provides a mountain retreat for city dwellers (about thirty miles west of Denver on I–70). Lots of specialty shops in a busy, but small-town atmosphere. Evergreen is surrounded by several mountain parks, and nearby Evergreen Lake is a favorite spot for visitors with boating in summer and ice skating in winter.

Many stars of the entertainment world have hideaway homes in the area. Downtown, take some time to visit the **Hiwan Homestead Museum,** a pioneer display in a seventeen-room log house. Included: a reconstructed 1880's assay office. Free tours in the afternoon, Tuesday through Sunday. Evergreen's surroundings of forests and meadows lend themselves to pleasant picnics and hikes.

Idaho Springs

Idaho Springs, above Evergreen on I–70, has been called "the buckle of Colorado's mineral belt." Families find a wealth of history here, and the community's hot springs—where the Ute Indians brought their old, sick, and wounded—are open year round.

Don't miss the **Clear Creek Museum** and the **Argo Gold Mill** downtown with equipment and mining displays inside an actual gold mine. There are tours of the shaft and adjoining ore mill, May through Labor Day. Small entrance fee.

Across the highway, via an underpass, is the **Indian Springs Resort.** Built in 1869, it is now a complete tourist facility—tennis courts, restaurants, and, of course, hot mineral baths.

The springs flow through two separate tunnels, one for men and one for women, carved into the mountains. You may wish to reserve a private bath for your family for an hour. Swimming pool, sauna, whirlpool are available, too. The dramatic **Bridal Veil Falls** is a short hike away.

It's difficult to top the nation's highest auto road—paved all the way—to the summit of Mt. Evans. (Follow the signs from town.) From 14,260 feet above sea level you can look down on passing clouds or see a sunrise. The Forest Service station at the base of the road (I–70 exit) can provide a tape and tape player for a self-guided tour of the peak. **Echo Lake,** also on the mountain, attracts anglers and overnight campers. (Skiers use the nearby XC trails in winter.)

For an adventurous side trip from Idaho Springs, drive up Fall River Road (Exit 48 from I–70) for an intimate look at various mountain terrains. The road ends at **St. Mary's Lake,** and a 30- or 40-minute climb up a well-marked footpath will bring you to St. Mary's Glacier, which has snow all year long. The glacier is popular with summer skiers.

Central City

Central City, once known as "the richest square mile on earth," is reached on Highway 119 via US 6 west from Golden. It was here, on a spot now marked by a modest plaque, where John Gregory first struck gold in 1859 and began the rush to the Rockies. In summer, Central City and its companion village of Blackhawk come alive, looking like reborn boom towns of a century ago. Winding Eureka Street sports saloons with swinging doors, gift shops, candy stores in a somewhat gaudy Old West manner. A great number of the brick buildings were erected in the old boom days. Likewise, some of the old mines still exist and can be inspected.

Some other attractions:

St. James Methodist Church on Eureka Street is the oldest Protestant edifice and oldest church in the state, dating back to 1859. The interior has just been restored; if the door is open, look in at the intricate stenciling which decorates the sanctuary.

The Teller House, 110 Eureka Street, was built in 1872 at the staggering cost of $107,000. It became the most opulent hostelry of the gold fields, hosting Ulysses S. Grant, Oscar Wilde, Baron de Rothschild, and other notables. In the saloon, visit the famous "Face on the Barroom Floor."

Central City is most renowned for its summer operas held in the old 1878 **Central City Opera House,** with solid stone walls four feet thick. Fine murals and crystal chandeliers decorate the Victorian interior. Artists from the New York Metropolitan Opera and other leading companies fly out on occasion to sing here. The operas are often followed by hit Broadway musicals and plays, frequently with the original casts. **The Lost Gold Mine** can be inspected a few blocks up the hill. (Small fee.)

Georgetown

Georgetown, just over fifty miles west of Denver along I–70, was named for George Griffith, the first prospector to strike gold there in 1860 at the confluence of the two streams at what now is 10th and Rose streets.

The discovery of silver after the gold played out gave Georgetown a continuing stability that other boomtowns lacked. Many miners built opulent Victorian mansions which have been preserved and added to the National Historic Register. Foremost among them is the **Hamill House,** 305 Argentine Street. Mining Czar William Hamill built it in the late 1870s; it is now almost completely restored and open for public tours. Two stone buildings on the back of the property served as Hamill's office and counting house. (The vault and curved walnut counter are still there.) Today, the buildings house the Georgetown Historical Society, a good stop for visitor information, brochures, and guides to area shops, restaurants, and attractions.

Four blocks away on 6th Street, in the commercial district, the **Hotel de Paris,** dating back to 1875, became famous throughout the West for its gourmet cuisine. Proprietor Louis DuPuy, a Frenchman, took fifteen years to complete the inn. When DuPuy died in 1900, it turned out that he was actually a French army deserter named Adolphe Gerard and had lived in Georgetown for thirty years under a false identity.

The hotel is open as a museum during the summer. (Noon to 4 P.M., closed Mondays.)

Unlike other old Colorado mining communities, Georgetown was never leveled by a major fire, thanks to the efficiency of its volunteer fire companies. Three of the antique fire houses still stand: the Alpine Hose Company on 5th Street, the Star Hook and Ladder (now the Georgetown municipal offices) on 6th Street, and Old Missouri, on Taos Street, across from Georgetown City Park.

You can also take a giant step backward in time and board the old Colorado and Southern narrow-gauge train that runs the four miles between Georgetown and Silver Plume. The line was a main supply route a hundred years ago. Now, visitors can make the forty-five-minute "loop"—so called because the track runs over and under itself repeatedly—on great bridges rising six hundred feet above the valley floor. The train stops at the Lebanon Mine for tours of the shaft and an adjoining museum. The trains run from Memorial Day through September.

HOTELS AND MOTELS

Rates for double occupancy average as follows: *Deluxe* $55–$100, *Expensive* $35–$54, *Moderate* $21–$34, *Inexpensive* $14–$20.

BOULDER

Best Western Boulder Inn. *Expensive.* 770 28th St. Across from University of Colorado. Restaurant, bar, pools, 100 attractively furnished rooms, private baths, own Chinese restaurant.

Best Western Golden Buff Motor Lodge. *Expensive.* 1725 28th St. Established motel convenient to University of Colorado campus. Large, well-decorated rooms, heated pool, exercise room, putting green.

The Broker Inn. *Expensive.* 555 30th. Near University of Colorado. Pool. Elegant Old West Restaurant on premises.

Hilton Harvest House Hotel. *Expensive.* 1345 28th St. A modern high-rise motel with landscaped grounds, dining facilities, cocktail lounge, swimming pool, 15 tennis courts. Recently enlarged. Shopping center nearby.

Holiday Inn of Boulder. *Expensive.* 800 28th St. Large national-chain motel. Pool, dining room.

Highlander Inn Motel. *Moderate.* 970 28th St. Pool. Near CU campus.

Hotel Boulderado. *Moderate.* Restored 1909 Victorian hotel with many antiques. Centrally located. Poet Robert Frost and other celebrities stayed here.

University Inn. *Moderate.* 1632 Broadway. Small, pleasant motel. Heated pool. Near downtown Boulder.

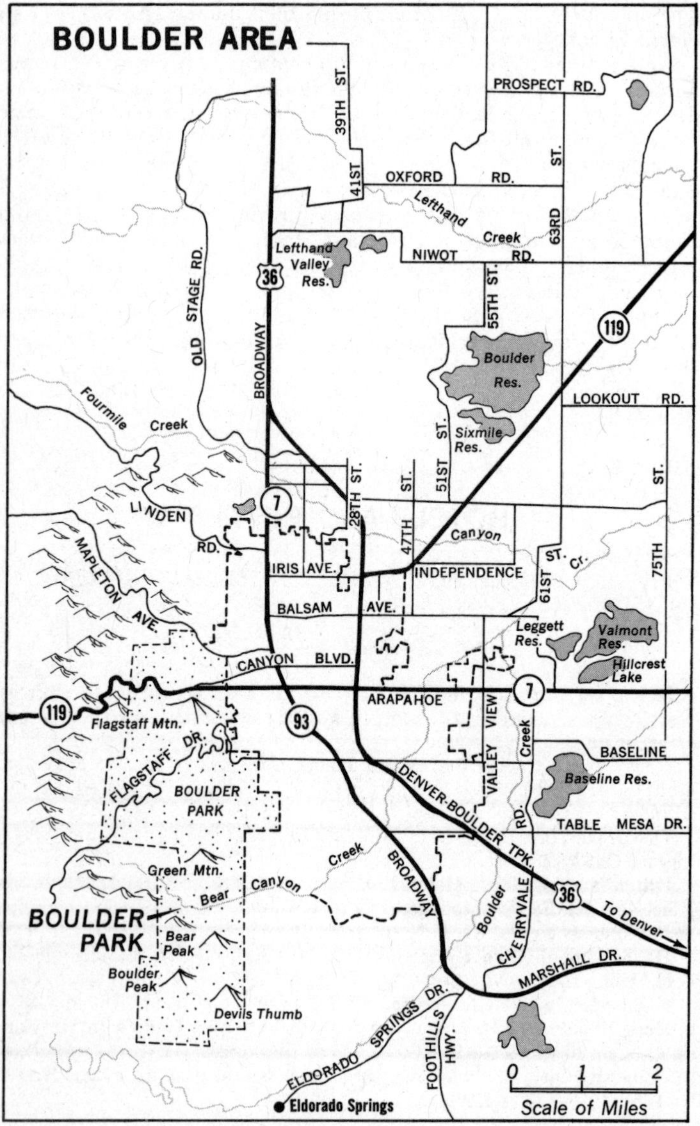
BOULDER AREA
PROSPECT RD.
39TH ST.
41ST
OXFORD RD.
63RD ST.
Lefthand Creek
NIWOT RD.
Lefthand Valley Res.
36
OLD STAGE RD.
BROADWAY
55TH ST.
119
Boulder Res.
LOOKOUT RD.
Fourmile Creek
Sixmile Res.
51ST ST.
47TH ST.
28TH ST.
75TH ST.
7
LINDEN RD.
MAPLETON AVE.
Canyon Cr.
IRIS AVE.
INDEPENDENCE
61ST ST.
BALSAM AVE.
Leggett Res.
Valmont Res.
Hillcrest Lake
CANYON BLVD.
ARAPAHOE
119
Flagstaff Mtn.
93
VALLEY VIEW
Creek
BASELINE
FLAGSTAFF DR.
BOULDER PARK
DENVER-BOULDER TPK.
Baseline Res.
TABLE MESA DR.
Green Mtn.
Bear Canyon Creek
BROADWAY
CHERRYVALE RD.
Boulder Creek
BOULDER PARK
Bear Peak
Boulder Peak
Devils Thumb
To Denver
MARSHALL DR.
ELDORADO SPRINGS DR.
FOOTHILLS HWY.
Eldorado Springs
0 1 2
Scale of Miles

Wagon Wheel Motel. *Inexpensive.* Four Mile Canyon, about 3 mi. from downtown. Just 17 rooms. Also on premises: campground with hookups.

CENTRAL CITY (Zip Code 80427)

Gilpin Hotel. *Moderate to Inexpensive.* Tiny, historic miners' hotel built in 1900 and well restored.

GEORGETOWN (80444)

Georgetown Motor Inn. *Moderate.* On east edge of town, I–70 exit 228. Alpine inn in a scenic, historic location. Restaurant, cocktail lounge.

GOLDEN (80401)

Holland House. *Moderate.* 1310 Washington Ave. On Golden's main street. Good location for mountain excursions. Has motel section, small café, bar. Clientele includes local mining engineers.

Golden Motel. *Inexpensive.* 24th at 4th St. Clean 15-unit motel.

IDAHO SPRINGS (80452)

Argo Motor Inn. *Expensive to Moderate.* Modernistic motel near mine. Tennis courts not far away. On river.

Indian Springs Resort. *Inexpensive.* Old resort hotel with mineral pool, baths, exercise room, small café. Off-trail and good value.

Peoriana Motel. *Inexpensive.* 1 mi. east on US 6, 40. Small, a favorite of skiers, has large, well-furnished rooms, café nearby.

EVERGREEN (80439)

Highland Haven Resort Motel. *Moderate.* Woodsy motel in forest on creek. Motel units, some with kitchenettes.

RESTAURANTS

Price categories for dinner, exclusive of drinks and tips are approximately: *Deluxe* $21 and up, *Expensive* $10–$20, *Moderate* $6–$9, *Inexpensive* below $6.

GOLDEN

Briarwood Inn. *Deluxe.* Elegant country Inn. Fine tablecloths, china, cutlery. Classical music background. Lazy Susan with free appetizers; great variety of American and Continental dishes. Each plate has visual appeal here. Always excellent dining experience.

BOULDER

Flagstaff House. *Deluxe.* On Flagstaff Mountain, offering fine views, award-winning Continental/American menu including own oven-smoked salmon, venison, filet a la Wellington, duck, Alaska king crab. Prime rib a specialty. Cocktail patio, free appetizers. Overlooks city, mountains. A treat in summer. Longtime owner Don Monette on premises.

Boulder Dinner Theatre. *Expensive.* 55th and Arapahoe. Cheerful young actors, singers, dancers regale you after a well-cooked supper.

Greenbriar Inn. *Expensive.* On US 36. Continental and American menu features veal Oscar, tournedos, shrimp Provençale. Own desserts. Old World atmosphere. Cocktail lounge.

Red Lion Inn. *Expensive.* Boulder Canyon Rd., 4 mi. west on State 119. Continental and American menu includes prime rib, elk, antelope, duck à l'orange. Cocktail lounge. Good wine list. Reservations required.

Berardi and Sons. *Moderate.* Popular Italian restaurant. Spicy food, bright lights. 2631 Broadway.

New York Delicatessen. *Moderate to Inexpensive.* 117 Pearl St. Good N.Y.-style Jewish delicatessen. Lunch and dinner. Open late on weekends.

Rudi's. *Moderate to Inexpensive.* 1831 Pearl. Natural foods, background music.

Furr's Cafeteria. *Inexpensive.* Iris St. and Hwy. 36. In large shopping center. Excellent value. No bar.

Tico's of Boulder. *Inexpensive.* 1101 Walnut St. Mexican and American menu. Cocktail lounge.

CENTRAL CITY

Black Forest Inn. *Expensive.* ¾ mi. east on State 279 in Black Hawk. A well-managed Bavarian restaurant. Authentic German dishes expertly prepared. Goose liver pâté, herring. Elk, venison, pheasant, and other native game featured. Wienerschnitzel, calves' liver à la Berlin, good trout, berries in season. Open noon to 9:30 P.M. Also for lunch. Beer Garden in summer. One of Colorado's more outstanding ethnic restaurants run by long-time owner-chef Bill Lorenz, a perfectionist. Closed Monday.

Teller House Eureka Room. *Expensive.* Laden with romance and history, the Teller House has been restored to its former splendor. Cocktail lounge. Teller Bar with "Face on the Bar Room Floor." Restaurant only open during summer.

EVERGREEN

El Rancho Colorado. *Expensive to Moderate.* Off I–70 exit 55A. In addition to steak and prime rib, always fresh, boned rainbow trout. The rustic atmosphere includes a terrace cocktail lounge with a fireplace. A pleasant restaurant in the heart of the mountains. Good value.

James Gang. *Moderate.* Upper Bear Creek Dr. Restaurant overlooks lake. Simple menu. Good values.

Dos Amigos. *Inexpensive.* Mexican café downtown.

IDAHO SPRINGS

Indian Springs Resort. *Moderate.* Home-cooking.

GEORGETOWN

Silver Queen Restaurant. *Expensive.* Victorian atmosphere, complete with cherrywood and stained glass. Varied menu.

EMPIRE

Peck House. *Expensive.* Distinguished restaurant in authentic Old West setting. Steak and trout specialties. En route to Berthoud Pass, Winter Park. Champagne brunch Sundays.

WINTER AND SUMMER RESORTS

Sun, Snow and Skyscrapers

The state which brought you Aspen and Vail, Winter Park and Steamboat Springs is renowned for its skiing. Justly so: Colorado has a greater number of major ski resorts and areas than other U.S. states or Canadian provinces. In all, you can ski at three dozen places that vary in size from giants like the Aspen complex to one-chairlift hills such as Idlewild. All these places appeal to non-skiers as well.

And keep in mind that the resorts operate summer programs, too.

Colorado attained an international reputation for its reliable snow conditions, sunshine aplenty, resorts en masse, good ski lodgings, restaurants, night life. Both eastern and western skiers enjoy the long descents and the variety of ski centers. Mountains of every kind!

Colorado serves the total novice, intermediate and expert, with ski schools ready to teach all ages in record time.

As a result, the Colorado ski business is terrific. Almost every season, after the figures are in, skier spending increases by 10 to 20 percent on the slopes, in the hostelries, and eateries, and bistros. Recessions never affected Colorado ski seasons, which produce from 5,200,000 to 9 million lift ticket sales per winter.

The aficionados arrive from all over the world, spanning all economic levels. A few ski vacationers are affluent while some midwestern couples may save all year for the same one-week ski fling.

The ski passions show up in places like Winter Park, an area owned by the City of Denver. The mountain is constantly polished by a motorized army of snowcats, graders, rollers, packers. Yet by Saturday or Sunday noon, the major runs are dotted with people. On holidays, thousands of Denverites come here in their own automobiles, in car pools, in chartered buses and via special weekend ski trains.

High-speed buses leave regularly from Stapleton International Airport, taking the traveler directly to the resorts. Large ski meccas such as Aspen or Vail have their own shuttle buses from lodges and condos to the lifts. And major complexes like Summit County which includes Breckenridge, Copper Mountain, Keystone, among others, are interconnected by shuttles. Likewise, air carriers cater to skiers. Continental Airlines, for instance, plans its flights with the winter sports crowd in mind, and Frontier and Trans-Colorado airlines jet to many mountain communities.

Which ski center should you pick? That depends on what you want. A traveler may opt for the prestige and urban big-city qualities of Vail, which nestles in a valley one hundred miles, or two hours, west of the Mile High City. An economy skier with a family may be drawn to Hidden Valley, which is operated by the Rocky Mountain National Park about seventy-six miles from Denver. A half-dozen major areas can be reached more quickly; each of these spots is different. Indeed, the flavor of Colorado's ski stations varies enormously. There are the former mining towns like Crested Butte, for example, and there are the sleek contemporary spas like Beaver Creek. Your choice will be influenced by many factors that include costs, types of slopes (from the gentlest to the raciest) and the kind of clientele you want to mix with. Some places—Winter Park, for instance—attract budget-conscious families more than the single jetsetter who favors the Aspen region.

Many travelers consider the closeness to Denver, too.

Departing from the Mile High City, here is an approximate sequence of resorts:

Loveland Basin

Loveland Basin was always one of the Denverites' favorite ski spots. And for ample reasons. "Loveland" (as Denverites call it) is close enough. Just fifty-five miles via I–70. No passes to cross. No need to drive through the Eisenhower Tunnel, either, which is "a big bore," according to Loveland's publicists.

The area therefore fetches visitors who can only spare a few days or a weekend. (For accommodations: see Georgetown and Keystone.) Denverites favor Loveland Basin's many fine bowls and wide trails, and the elbow room. In a sense, Loveland's terrain reminds one of the Swiss Alps; it is very scenic.

Loveland Basin's ski action takes place at 12,300 feet, which results in one of the state's longest ski seasons, usually until the first of May. (Thanks to snowmaking equipment, the area already gets started in October.) One small disadvantage: there are no accommodations at the ski area itself. You'll have to commute.

Winter Park

A ski center sixty-seven miles west of Denver via US 40, Winter Park has begun to catch up with Colorado's big-time resorts. It all started during the mid-seventies when Winter Park more than doubled its skier capacity by adding four long chairlifts and a whole new "Mary Jane" mountain. Now there are fifteen lifts and almost one hundred runs.

The ski resort offers more than the comfortable, rustic ski lodges for which it became known; there are luxurious condos as well.

During the late seventies, this popular family resort added many restaurants. And ski lodges serve solid meals because guests stay on the American plan. Many of the inns feature whirlpools, saunas, indoor swimming, Ping-Pong, sleigh rides, skating. Through the years, Winter Park's reputation was built mostly by families.

Many of Denver's adults learned to ski here when they were children, and this still holds true for the present-day pre-school generation. The chairlift crews at this area traditionally show much patience with people who only ski a couple of times a season, or use the lifts just for a few days a year. The operators automatically slow down the machinery for first-timers, tyros, or the many small children.

Winter Park moved up into the big leagues not just because of its many satellite activities and diversions, but on the basis of its immense layout, which spans four mountains. Although the vertical drop may be less than that of Aspen, the resort encourages skiing for every kind of person, on packed super runs, "boulevards," trails and forest paths, and chutes with untouched powder snow. The Mary Jane slopes favor the expert. In summer, the resort reverts to dude ranching, horseback riding, organized hikes, and art fairs, among other activities.

Ski Idlewild

Nearby Ski Idlewild caters to the person who has never skied before, and to the "little bit" skier. The total vertical rise amounts to a mere four hundred feet. The four runs are short, and the terrain is so wide that it cannot arouse anxieties in even the shyest of first-timers. You can rent equipment and arrange for lessons at the base lodge. The area has much cross-country skiing, too. After the snow melts, the lodge caters to trout anglers and riders.

Arapahoe Basin

Arapahoe Basin can be reached via I–70 through the Eisenhower Tunnel. Some of the area's most delightful periods are late April and May, when you see few people here. Indeed, despite its magnificent alpine vista, this fine mountain somehow doesn't attract great masses.

Arapahoe Basin works for budgeteers; you notice a lot of skiers who wear jeans, farmer's overalls, knickers, cotton shirts, dime-store sweaters, windbreakers, and even army jackets. None of that expensive high-style fashion you spot in Vail. Rock climbing is available here in late summer.

Keystone

The handsome, well-planned Keystone Resort is seventy-five miles west of Denver via I–70, and five miles down the road from Arapahoe Basin, which is owned by the same corporation as the Keystone Resort.

Keystone has much in its favor. First of all, there is an impressive hotel, which cost $9 million to build and has all the luxury touches. (You can also check into small and large condos or a motel; see *Dillon* listings.) Secondly, there is the pleasant, ever-expanding Keystone Village, complete with varied restaurants, boutiques, shops, diversions, other sports activities that include a Gardiner indoor tennis setup. Most important, perhaps, the resort features simpatico slopes aimed at the average recreational skier with plenty of room for the beginner.

Keystone seems ideal if you are a ski tourist in search of conservation. The runs here were hardly tampered with; so you still get the feel of nature among the spruce, the fir and the balsam. The trail designers used the terrain to perfection, leaving the lodge pole pines at various junctures, and making the most of the natural glades. Like most of

Colorado's ski resorts, Keystone also has many summer activities. Keystone's skaters' lake then switches to boaters. Condos, lodge, restaurants and other facilities well-connected via a free shuttle.

Copper Mountain

The Copper Mountain ski terrain swoops from a base elevation of 9,600 feet above sea level to summits at 12,050 feet; separate runs for all skiing skills aren't a PR-invention but a reality. The area's forty miles of *pistes* actually fulfill the needs of every type of skier who share the slopes by peers, not competitors.

For example, you at once notice an especially tame, extra-wide mountain for the timid or the beginner. Directly overlooking the base facilities, you see longer intermediate runs for those who've already tried the sport. The experts command an almost three thousand vertical drop at the other end of Copper's spectrum. Races are held there.

Most skiers spend the night in apartment house-like condominiums. Copper is also known for its Club Med, a French vacation village which only accepts week-long guests. The Saturday-Sunday-holiday influx of skiers by the thousands from Denver and Colorado, plus ski tourists from elsewhere, along with the Club Med invasion all make for occasionally crowded slopes. Club Med shuts down in summer, but Copper offers a lively tennis program plus relaxation by the swimming pools.

Breckenridge

Breckenridge awaits in the same general vicinity as Copper Mountain. (Both are located in Summit County.) The distance to Breckenridge is seventy-four miles from Denver via I–70 and Colo 9.

The town of Breckenridge is typically Coloradan; it has all the right traces of mining (gold began in 1858; silver, in 1878), and all the right Old West bars and cafés. The Aspen Skiing Corporation operates skiing facilities. Accommodations generally consist of town houses and forest-surrounded condominiums.

Breckenridge appeals to families, especially those from the East and Midwest. Most of the ski runs are fairly short but well maintained. The overall atmosphere is pleasant Old West. Nonskiers can browse in the many shops. Nice for a typical Old Western summer vacation, too.

Vail

Vail began in 1962 as a small alpine-style village with one ski lodge, a few restaurants, and some modest condos. Its 110-mile distance from the Colorado capital didn't deter the number of ski tourists who flock here. Indeed, the remoteness added to Vail's magnetism for the Beautiful People, the Jet Set, and the Very Very Rich.

Vail has a corner on the "International" flavor (the Vail bank even changes foreign currency). Foreign languages are spoken, you will find many restaurants of Austrian, Swiss, German, and French extraction. You share all this with diplomats, young wealthy business executives, actresses, flight attendants and fashion buyers. Oil and stock tycoons, politicians, U.S. government cabinet members, models, and "Playmates" ski these slopes along with well-to-do Texans. Shops sell imported $2,000 fur coats, French champagnes, Swiss watches, Irish Linen, and all manner of fine Danish and Dutch cheeses. You'll find almost anything in this complete village, which even boasts a ski museum, a movie theater, and several supermarkets. In short, Vail is the most chic and most expensive area in Colorado.

The daily tab for lifts has risen to astronomical heights. The yearly increases don't seem to lessen the lift queues: on a typical Sunday, this famous ski mecca may draw 15,000 skiers. A gondola accident some seasons ago caused the deaths of several skiers and the injury of others. The guilty lift has been rebuilt and is now safe.

Vail is one of the few Colorado resorts where you also stand in lines at restaurants, where reservations at lodges are often difficult to get, and where the day skier must pay for parking. Illegally parked vehicles are quickly whisked away by the Vail police, and motorists must pay heavy tow charges and fines to recapture their vehicles. (Advice: arrive by bus.)

Vail has changed as a community. It is a big town now. Density is high. Pollution has begun. (In winter, some 4,000 fireplaces belch much smoke.) The growth of condo-skyscrapers, parking garages for 1,200 cars, the hundreds of shops and businesses, the very bigness makes Vail a different, less intimate place from the Vail of the late sixties. It is still worth a visit, however, and satisfies many of its ski fans. After all, it is the single largest ski area in the state and its alpine "bowl" skiing cannot be duplicated in Colorado. In summer, Vail offers tennis, golf, horseback riding, swimming and many more activities.

Beaver Creek

Beaver Creek, located eight miles west of Vail, and owned-operated by Vail Associates, must be considered the important, best-planned Colorado ski resort of the 1980s. Many millions of dollars have already been spent on land and ski area development, on base facilities and roads, with another $500 million to be spent in years to come. The chairlifts are in, serving almost 560 acres. The shuttle runs from Vail to the sister village's well-groomed slopes. Vertical drop is 3,280 feet.

Condominium and lodge accommodations available. Beaver Creek is recommended to skiers who appreciate quiet, uncluttered slopes. In summer, Beaver Creek offers golfing, horses, river rafting, and jeep tours.

Aspen

Aspen is still Colorado's ski giant. It has been called the "Capital of Colorado Ski Country USA," the "Big Granddaddy of Resorts," a "Pantheon of Skiing." To one authority, it is the "best all-round American ski place." Actually, Aspen *is* the biggest ski mecca in North America. It consists of four huge mountains, each with its own atmosphere and style. Over 250 miles of trails crisscross this incredible resort complex.

Aspen deserves the accolades. The assorted slopes please all comers, from timid beginner to bold intermediate, to super expert, from racer to first-timer.

Choices! There is Aspen mountain, which rises above and towers over the town, Aspen Highlands with its spectacular views and deeply plunging runs, and a short distance away, Buttermilk Mountain (which has the most gentle terrain), and lastly, the more contemporary development, Snowmass-at Aspen. Here you will find a change of pace. Apart from to-your-door skiing, Snowmass offers ice skating, ski touring and dog sledding.

The Aspen slopes get busy but the skiers seem to scatter across the region. Some of the people patronize the motel facilities distributed through the valley or they ski Snowmass and stay there in the condominium-lodges. The village acreage provides elbow room for the buildings that slant up the slopes. Trees greet outside the windows; small creeks and paths meander down Snowmass' Tibetan tiers. Snowmass has unity, sanity, forethought.

There are hostelries at the base of Aspen Highlands, under the Buttermilk ski area, at Little Nell and up toward Independence Pass and below big Aspen Mountain, once known as Ajax Mountain.

Over the past decade, downtown Aspen has improved its looks. At one core area is a handsome pedestrian mall with flower boxes and benches. Moreover, Aspen's red Old West brick buildings and the Victorian gingerbread homes were periodically restored. The antique cherry wood bars shine, as do the new Tiffany lamps and the stained-glass windows. Green plants grace many Aspen stores and cafés. Aspen outranks most North American ski resorts when it comes to the sheer number and variety of restaurants and night-life possibilities. There are more than one hundred-plus spots where one can dine, or have lunch. Aspen has bistros, bars, saloons, pubs, subterranean dives, cafeterias, cafés, pastry shops, coffee shops, and several internationally famous restaurants. A cosmopolitan, polyglot, manifold town. Aspen is everything to every skier, and happily, to every nonskier as well; the town seems ideal for singles, couples or families. Several hundred shops invite browsers; amusements and sports of every kind beckon.

In summer, Aspen holds an important music festival as well as conferences. (See details about Aspen's summer season in *The Rest of the State.*)

There are some negative aspects to this large resort. Traffic is heavy. Winter reservations are hard to come by. Prices during the ski season have risen to formidable heights at even the most average motels. And while direct air connections from Denver via feeder airlines is available, you pay top dollar for the thirty-five minute flight to Aspen. (Reserve your seat long in advance.)

Steamboat Springs

Steamboat Springs can be reached by air from Stapleton International or by automobile via I–70 and Route 40 from Denver. The 163-mile drive across Berthoud and Rabbit Ears passes takes you about 3½ hours, and possibly 5. The spaciousness visible along the route extends to Mount Werner (10,600 feet high) and to Thunderhead Mountain, on which you ski many easy slopes and some difficult ones. Steamboat gives great enjoyment to the beginning skier, with uncluttered, extra-easy, well-packed acres for novices. The outstanding lift network includes 15 chairlifts plus gondola. Snowmaking ensures an early season.

Steamboat Springs is a happy combination of classic old ski town, a modern well-financed ski resort, and a lucky blend of long season, and lodging to suit every pocketbook. Things work out nicely here for average families, for couples, and for singles. Steamboat is also a pleasant mountain town in summer. Horseback riders, anglers, hikers, backpackers enjoy it greatly from June to early October.

Crested Butte and Other Ski Places

Crested Butte is 228 miles southwest from Denver. The driving distance makes for an absence of lift lines. Few Denverites come here. Frontier and Trans-Colorado airlines connect with Gunnison, Crested Butte's gateway. You'll find these spectacular mountains fairly untrammeled. But don't come during the college vacation.

The mountain of Crested Butte is connected to the old mining town by a free shuttle bus. In addition to the downhill skiing, the resort has a fine cross-country school and trail system. Most lodgings are more modestly priced than at the huge ski meccas.

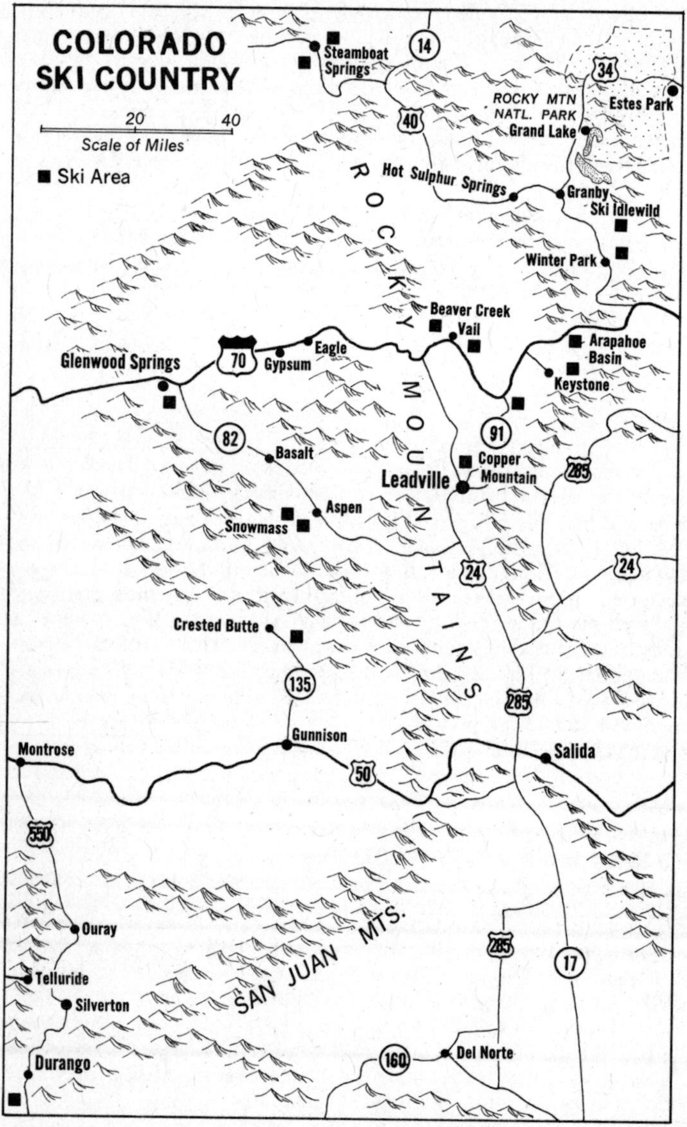
COLORADO
SKI COUNTRY
20
40
Scale of Miles
■ Ski Area
Steamboat Springs
14
34
40
ROCKY MTN NATL. PARK
Estes Park
Grand Lake
Hot Sulphur Springs
Granby
Ski Idlewild
Winter Park
ROCKY MOUNTAINS
Beaver Creek
Vail
Arapahoe Basin
Keystone
Glenwood Springs
70
Gypsum
Eagle
82
91
Basalt
Copper Mountain
Leadville
285
Aspen
Snowmass
24
24
Crested Butte
135
285
Gunnison
Montrose
Salida
50
550
Ouray
SAN JUAN MTS.
285
17
Telluride
Silverton
Durango
160
Del Norte

Relaxation is possible at this remote resort. Likewise, Telluride, located 327 road miles from Denver gateway—Durango—appeals to the get-away-from-it-all skier. Telluride's scenery is spectacular. Colorado also features many smaller ski places, such as Lake Eldora, Sunlight, Purgatory, Monarch, Wolf Creek, Hidden Valley, and Tamarron, which are all worth investigating. For more information on the Colorado areas and resorts, write to: Colo. Ski Country USA, 1410 Grant St., Denver, CO 80203.

Silver Creek

Silver Creek is the state's newest ski center. Located off Highway 40 near Granby, the area consists of several pleasant mountains for all types of skiers, a Ramada resort hotel, a gourmet restaurant, coffee shops, ski shops, and a health club. Recommended for families in search of a peaceful and simple holiday.

Cross-Country Skiing

Colorado has also become one of the nation's most important centers for ski touring, or "XC-skiing." Special ski lodges, guest ranches, and instructors cater to the aficionado of this quiet winter activity. Among the leading places are the *Peaceful Valley Ski Touring Center* in Lyons; the *Ski Idlewild Lodge* at Winter Park, *Devil's Thumb Ranch* in nearby Fraser; Steamboat Springs *Ski Corporation Ski Touring Center; Copper Mountain Ski Escape Touring School,* the *Tamarron Resort XC* program near Durango; the *Nordic Adventure Ski Touring Center* and *Ambush Ranch* in Crested Butte; and *Silver Creek,* (10 kilometers of free trails). *Rocky Mountain Ski Tours,* Box 413, Estes Park, 80517, can lead you into the more remote areas of The Rocky Mountain National Park.

HOTELS AND MOTELS

Rates based on double occupancy average as follows (though they may vary depending on the season): *Deluxe* $65–$120, *Expensive* $45–$64, *Moderate* $30–$44, *Inexpensive* below $30.

ASPEN (Zip Code 81611)

(Winter reservations needed many weeks in advance.)
Aspen Chateaux. *Deluxe.* Condos.

Aspen Meadows. *Deluxe.* West edge of town. This large complex offers accommodations with central building containing all hotel services, plus health center, saunas, steam baths, tennis courts, swimming pool, cocktail lounge. Shuttle service to town and slopes.

The Gant. *Deluxe.* Condominium hotel. Heated pool, lawn games, skiing, health club, conference rooms, bar, entertainment.

Pomegranate Inn. *Deluxe.* 2 mi. west on State 82. Excellent location for Buttermilk Skiing. Rooms with fireplaces, suites, heated pool and therapy pool, ice cream parlor, billiard room. Restaurant.

Tipple Inn. *Deluxe.* Centrally located luxury condos. Restaurant, cocktail bar.

Wildwood Inn. *Deluxe.* Elegant, well-appointed hostelry in Snowmass. Open summer and winter only.

Holiday Inn. *Deluxe to Expensive.* At foot of Buttermilk Mountain. Open all year. Good location for skiers.

Snowmass Resort Lodges and Condominiums. *Deluxe to Expensive.* Quality accommodations in idyllic Snowmass Village, directly on slopes. Relaxing and luxurious. Write Snowmass Resort Assn., Snowmass Village, Colo. 81615.

Jerome Hotel. *Expensive.* Famous restored old hotel on Main St. Not all rooms have bath. A Victorian relic. Bar. Café.

Maroon Creek Lodge. *Expensive.* 2½ mi. southwest on Maroon Creek Rd. Car advisable. Early American decor. Units with living room, kitchenette, bath, and one or two bedrooms. Heated pool, sauna. Spectacular view. Remote.

Prospector. *Expensive.* E. Hyman at S. Monarch. A small, long-established, informal. Breakfast included in daily rates. Heated pool.

Ullr Lodge. *Expensive.* 520 West Main Street. Good for budget-conscious skiers and summer travelers.

BRECKENRIDGE (80424)

Beaver Run. *Deluxe.* Large condo complex. Convention facilities, health club, restaurant, cocktail lounges. Directly at base of ski lifts.

Tannhäuser. *Deluxe.* Condominiums for larger groups. Maid service.

Breckenridge Inn and Resort. *Expensive.* Two-story motel with café and bar. Tennis in summer.

COPPER MOUNTAIN (80443)

Copper Mountain Resort Assn. *Deluxe to Expensive.* Many skyscraper-condo apartments. Write Box 1, Copper Mountain, Colo. 80443.

Club Mediterranée. *Expensive.* Lodge for week-long ski vacations. Rates include excellent meals and accommodations, ski lessons, lift tickets, entertainment. Young, active crowd. Club has an 800 number.

CRESTED BUTTE (81224)

Crested Butte Lodge. *Deluxe.* At the ski area. Heated pool, sauna, playground, pets limited in this luxurious modern lodge. Summer activities as well as skiing in winter.

Nordic Inn. *Expensive.* Directly on slopes. Some kitchen units. Lovely, Norwegian-style, complimentary continental breakfast, hot tub/Jacuzzi, cable T.V., friendly proprietor, cross-country ski tours, and summer activities. Highly recommended.

Elk Mountain Lodge. *Inexpensive.* Simple accommodations. Budget restaurant. Good value.

DILLON (80435)

Lake Dillon Condotel. *Deluxe.* Adjacent to lake. Whirlpool.

Ramada-Silverthorne. *Expensive.* Large motor hotel; ideal location close to major ski areas, and summer recreation. Some super-large units. Large indoor pool. Sauna. Good restaurant and bar. Disco. Winter and summer packages available. A good spot for Copper Mountain skiers.

Super 8. *Moderate.* Well-known no-frills chain motel.

KEYSTONE (80435)

Keystone Resort. *Deluxe.* Elegant European-style, low-slung hotel with many luxury touches. Skiing at doorstep. Indoor-outdoor pool for year-round use. French restaurant. Café. Shops in village. Delightful lakeside location for summer. Well-managed and classy. All sports. Year-round Gardiner Tennis Ranch. Deluxe condos in addition to hotel rooms. (Near Dillon.)

STEAMBOAT SPRINGS (80477)

Sheraton at Steamboat (formerly, Steamboat Village Inn). *Deluxe to Expensive.* Directly at ski area. Skyscraper hotel with condos, convention facilities, restaurants, golf, tennis.

Bear Claw. *Deluxe.* Plush mountaintop condo complex for a demanding clientele.

Holiday Inn. *Expensive.* 3 mi. east on US 40. Two stories, attractive, some balconies. Heated pool, kennel, sauna, restaurant and cocktail lounge. 24-hour coffeeshop. Bar.

Best Western Ptarmigan Inn. *Expensive.* 2 mi. east on US 40. Attractive motel located directly under Mt. Werner. Heated pool, sauna, restaurant and cocktail lounge.

Ramada. *Expensive.* On Hwy. 40. All facilities.

Best Western Alpiner. *Expensive to Moderate.* On Hwy. # 40 downtown. Well-established motel.

Super 8. *Expensive to Moderate.* At Hwy. 40 and Mt. Werner Rd. Chain motel.

Harbor Hotel. *Inexpensive.* Old, restored, downtown hotel, with modest restaurant, Western bar. Bus stops here.

Nite's Rest Motel. *Inexpensive.* Small, family-owned.

VAIL (81657)

Holiday Inn-at Vail. *Deluxe.* A $5-million skier's motel with every kind of accommodation, from condos to smaller rooms. Free parking for guests.

Lodge at Vail. *Deluxe.* Splendid alpine lodge with spacious rooms, restaurant, sauna, cocktail lounge, large heated pool.

Marriott's Mark Resort. *Deluxe.* A 228-room super-hotel–health-club with penthouse restaurant, shops, conference center. Located at Lion's Head.

Westin Hotel Vail. *Deluxe.* New $50 million resort complex.

Roost Lodge. *Expensive to Moderate.* Motel on outskirts of Vail.

Vail Village Inn. *Expensive.* 1 block north of I–70. Large motor inn. Olympic outdoor pool, coffee shop, cocktail lounge, fireplace lounge, sun decks, good location. Close to bus stop. Free parking for guests.

WINTER PARK (80482)

Hi Country Haus Resort. *Deluxe.* Spacious condominiums, recreation center, indoor pool; large groups in winter. Cross-country skiing. Free shuttle to ski area. Own rafts. Grocery store, cafés, movie theater on premises. Meeting room for 120 persons.

Beaver's Lodge and Beaver Village. *Expensive.* Lodge rooms and condos. Soundproofed walls, handsome stone fireplaces. Excellent meals included. Dude ranch in summer. Well-known complex.

Hi Country Inn. *Expensive.* Best Western Lodge with bubble-protected all-year pool, sauna, game rooms, bar, quality food. Summer programs. Skiing close by.

Meadow Ridge Resort Condominiums. *Expensive.* 10 minutes west of Winter Park on hillside. Remote and idyllic. Good for large families, groups, honeymooners. Swimming pool. Tennis courts. Free shuttle to skiing.

Sitzmark Ski Lodge and Guest Ranch. *Expensive.* Well-run establishment with small clean rooms, friendly atmosphere. Near two ski areas, free shuttles.

Idlewild Guest Ranch & Lodge. *Expensive to Moderate.* Long-established enclave with its own ski hill, ski lifts, simple accommodations, rustic bar, meals for ski week and dude ranch guests. Cross-country facility in winter. Off-trail. Summer activities include fishing, horseback rides, hiking.

Miller's Inn. *Moderate.* Ski lodge with family-style meals and varied accommodations.

RESTAURANTS

Restaurant categories for dinner, exclusive of drinks and tips, are approximate: *Deluxe* $25 and up, *Expensive* $12–$25, *Moderate* $8–$12, *Inexpensive* below $8.

ASPEN

Copper Kettle. *Deluxe.* Each night authentic dishes from a different nation or area are featured. Cocktail lounge. Reservation. *Prix fixe.* Not for those on a budget.

Crystal Palace. *Deluxe.* Victorian decor. The steak dinners accompanied by Broadway shows are good. Cocktail lounge. Reservations difficult to obtain in winter.

Andre's. *Deluxe to Expensive.* International menu. Well-known for breakfasts and lunches, too.

Chart House. *Expensive.* Steaks and crab. Large salad bar. Excellent value. Cocktail lounge.

Guido's Swiss Inn. *Expensive.* A Swiss chalet under Aspen Mountain with much to offer.

La Reserve. *Expensive.* At Snowmass. Elegant restaurant with European atmosphere. Swiss chef. Recommended.

Mother Lode. *Expensive to Moderate.* 316 E. Hyman. Longtime Italian ristorante. Cozy.

Arthur's Chinese Restaurant. *Moderate.* On West Main St. Solid Oriental cooking in Victorian atmosphere. Bar. No reservations accepted.

The Steakhouse at Skiers Chalet. *Moderate.* Aspen St. at #1 lift. Good for families, this candlelit restaurant overlooks the town and mountain. Charcoal-broiled steaks.

Stewpot. *Moderate to Inexpensive.* An American goulash place in Snowmass.

BRECKENRIDGE

Briar Rose. *Expensive.* Victorian 1890s décor on the site of an old mining boardinghouse. Specialty is steak. Good crab legs. Own saloon.

Weber's. *Expensive.* Good German cooking.

El Perdido. *Moderate.* Well-known Mexican fare. Margaritas and vinos.

COPPER MOUNTAIN

Farley's. *Expensive.* From steaks to scampi. A little noisy and cramped.

CRESTED BUTTE

Jeremiah's. *Expensive.* Hearty breakfasts and varied dinners at base of mountain.

Le Bosquet French Restaurant. *Expensive.* Frog legs' Provencale, fresh trout with salmon mousse, rabbit chasseur, and other French specialties. Wines. Cozy atmosphere. Lunches, too.

Soupçon. *Expensive.* Ambitious Continental fare.

The Elk Mountain Dining Room. *Inexpensive.* Delicious Mexican food, friendly staff.

DILLON

Alf's Gasthof Bavaria. *Deluxe to Expensive.* Truly Bavarian restaurant. Schnitzel, spaetzle, sauerbraten all genuine. Black Forest torte. Children's portions. Gemütlich. Nightly entertainment.

La France Restaurant. *Expensive.* Chef-owned, authentic French country cooking. 5 entrées. *Prix fixe.* Good wines. Genuine French atmosphere. Fireplace.

KEYSTONE

Garden Room. *Deluxe.* Plus French restaurant in Keystone Lodge. Authentic. For finicky palates. Elegant china and glassware.

The Ranch. *Deluxe.* Dining at rustic ranch house. Flawless service, cozy fireplace atmosphere.

Navigator. *Deluxe to Expensive.* A complete fish restaurant in the Rockies.

Bighorn Steakhouse. *Expensive.* Good salad bar and drinks. At Keystone Lodge.

STEAMBOAT SPRINGS

Remington's. *Deluxe.* In the Sheraton at Steamboat. Exhaustive menu with the unusual—venison, buffalo, fresh fish—plus the more expected meat and fowl.

Cipriani's. *Expensive.* Superb Italian restaurant. Many innovative dishes. One of the best in the state. Italian wines.

The Brandywine. *Expensive to Moderate.* An old restaurant filled with antiques and plants. Simple menu, good cooking. Drinks.

The Cove. *Expensive to Moderate.* True Cantonese cooking at Harbor Hotel. Highly recommended.

Mazzola's Italian Restaurant. *Inexpensive.* Good for the budget conscious. Late dinner hours.

VAIL

Gasthof Gramshammer. *Deluxe.* Austrian menu. Tyrolean atmosphere. Antlers Room features rack of venison, elk steak, children's plates, all at high prices. Outdoor café. Open all year.

Clock Tower Inn. *Deluxe to Expensive.* Mostly prime rib, steaks, crab.

Left Bank. *Expensive.* Genuine French restaurant. Coq au vin especially recommended. Reservations essential long in advance. Closed Oct. to mid-Nov.

Watch Hill Oyster Club. *Expensive.* Long list of fish appetizers. Fresh fish flown in daily. Pleasant ambiance.

Frasiers. *Expensive to Moderate.* Cozy restaurant-saloon at Lion's Head. Good meats. Ask for daily specials. Busy at lunch. Open until 11 P.M. Recommended.

WINTER PARK

The Hideaway. *Deluxe.* Continental fare in an intimate candlelight setting. Good service. Elegant and expensive. Classical music. Small. Reservations essential.

Portobello Road. *Deluxe to Expensive.* Hwy. 40, at the Ramada, Silver Creek. Unexpected gourmet headquarters: veal Oscar, picatta, quail, chateaubriand.

Chalet Restaurant. *Moderate.* Ambitious Continental fare, with some American items and crêpes. Chef-owned. Good open wines. Friendly and reliable. Lunches, too. Closed Monday.

Club Car. *Moderate.* Western restaurant at Mary Jane area, operated by Winter Park. Good appetizer selection. Steaks, plus fowl and some fish. Efficient bar. Restaurant opens only at peak winter and summer periods. Recommended.

Hi Country Inn. *Moderate.* Excellent American food. Prime rib a specialty. Excellent salads. Pleasant bar. Reservations needed.

The Shed. *Moderate to Inexpensive.* Large menu. Excellent American food and large portions. Be prepared to wait 40 to 60 minutes to get seated during ski season. Slow service does not seem to diminish popularity with skiers.

Hernando's Pizza. *Inexpensive.* Pizza, spaghetti, and other Italian food at almost all hours. Good value. Beer and wine.

L.C. Benedict. *Inexpensive.* Everything from eggs benedict for breakfast to good chicken dinners. Cozy Colonial setting. Often closes before 8:30 P.M. Good value.

ROCKY MOUNTAIN NATIONAL PARK

A Town Named Estes Park

Only a tenderfoot looks for a park at Estes Park. "Park" is an old western term for a mountain valley, and this was Joel Estes' domain in 1860. When two other families moved in to share this huge, rugged hollow in the Rockies, Estes moved out, complaining of "too many" people. Although the mountain village has a permanent population of just a few thousand, each summer it hosts more than two million visitors thanks to the surrounding mountains and to the famous Rocky Mountain National Park.

After Joel Estes moved on, the British visitor Lord Dunraven attempted to establish a private preserve here. F.O. Stanley of the steamer fame came next. Thanks to him, Estes Park became a tourist town that serves the mountain traveler.

Most tourists begin their visit at the **Visitors' Center** at the south edge of town, at the intersections of Highways 34, 36, and 7. The staff of ten keeps it open seven days a week in summer. Slide presentations on the region's natural history and on area activities are available. You can also check schedules for sightseeing tours.

Among Estes Park's features: the eighteen- and nine-hole golf courses, both challenging to play. The eighteen-hole course, located just one mile from downtown on Highway 7, has a pro shop, snack shop, driving range, rental bags, clubs, pull and electric carts, and all other equipment. The nine-hole course, located just east of the Visitor Center on Highway 34, is also next to the Big Thompson River and Lake Estes. Electric carts can be rented only at the eighteen-hole course.

At Lake Estes you will find rental boats, boat docks, tackle shop, snack shop, and other boating and fishing needs.

The District-owned tennis courts are available free both day and night. There are two lighted courts at night (small charge). Other courts are located in Stanley Park on Community Drive.

The Recreation District maintains many picnic areas along Lake Estes, Mary's Lake, and Stanley Park. Also available is a children's playground in Stanley Park near the tennis and basketball courts.

Sightseeing

The **Estes Park Aerial Tramway,** on Moraine Park Road, carries passengers to the 8,896-foot summit of Prospect Mountain for an unmatched look at the community and surrounding mountains. It's a short ride. Mid-May through mid-September.

The **Estes Park Area Historical Museum,** downtown on Elkhorn Avenue, relives the history of the region through photos, artifacts, and documents. Open daily, May through September.

The (modest) **MacGregor Ranch Museum,** half-mile north of downtown on Devil's Gulch Road, preserves the hundred-year life of a working cattle ranch. MacGregor's first cabin and the 1896 farmhouse display tools, clothes, and other memorabilia of the owners and their times. Open Memorial Day through Labor Day, closed Monday.

The **Movie and TV Wax Museum** features a collection of motion picture history. Exhibits include wax figures, props, and costumes. Also pictures and continuous showings of old films; more than two thousand original movie posters. Daily, mid-May through mid-September, downtown at 125 Moraine Avenue.

Ripley's Believe It Or Not Museum pays homage to the bizarre in exhibits drawn from the famous newspaper feature. Elkhorn Avenue at US 34, open May through August.

Shops attract plenty of summer trade. At the **Centennial Park** (on West Elkhorn), you'll find hand-made goods, a sidewalk café, carvings made from native aspens, and a unique clock tower that turns like a music box figure as it chimes. Estes Park stores also offer complete outdoor, hiking, camping, and mountaineering equipment at slightly higher rates than those of Denver. Most of the businesses are closed in late fall, winter, and spring.

Rocky Mountain National Park

The resort town of Estes Park is "base camp" for each year's 2½ million-plus visitors to the Rocky Mountain National Park. The National Park's 266,943 acres (or 417 square miles) straddle the Continental Divide.

Both entrances to the park have complete visitors' centers. Here you can get detailed maps and information on outings, activities, backcountry permits, camping, and a free movie about the park. (Backpackers must register here.) Nature walks and talks by park rangers offer personalized educational and wildlife experiences for the whole family. The Rocky Mountain National Park programs begin in early June and extend into September. There are also some self-guided trails.

To acquaint yourself with the area, take a day or more to drive its very safe and well-maintained roads. The main route is via Trail Ridge Road, which connect Estes Park with Grand Lake. The famous highway rises and descends, curves and straightens or turns into serpentines for many hours and miles. It is the longest continuous such paved mountain road in North America. At several points, the route reaches and stays at twelve thousand-foot levels. Yet the driving is quite manageable for flatlanders.

Trail Ridge is open only after it has been cleared of snow, usually from June through Labor Day. You need no special tires or mountain driving expertise. Caution is necessary for the eleven miles you're above timberline, in a world of dwarfed, wind-carved trees and alpine tundra jeweled with miniature flowers. American elk and mule deer sometimes graze in the upper meadows. From the lookout at the highway's topmost point, 12,183 feet, the vistas weave in all directions. Frozen lakes, formed by the slow sculpturing of the ice, gleam at the foot of glacial moraines. From near the summit you can see Iceberg Lake with its ever-present glacial surface. Dress warmly for this drive.

Visit the **Alpine Visitor Center.** The exhibits will help you understand some of the things you have seen along the way.

The entire highway is lined with unforgettable sights: Jackstraw Mountain, where huge trees burned in an 1872 forest fire still lie like bleached bones: the Never Summer Mountains with their eternal snows; and Moraine Park, where an ancient glacier began to form the area. Most park entrances have booths that rent cassettes and cassette players to give you an expertly guided self-tour of the entire area.

Another route: the original Fall River Road, built in 1920. Because of the steep grades and many switchbacks, this road is not open to trailers and motorized vans.

If you have an extra hour, you may also wish to explore Bear Lake Road, just nine miles long. It begins at the Moraine Park Visitors' Center, and ends at Bear Lake, one of the most spectacular sights at the park. The lake area offers a panorama of glaciers, mountain peaks, forests, and streams. Above Bear Lake lie several other beautiful lakes. Hiking trails connect you with Dream Lake.

A note on driving in the park: speed limits and traffic laws are enforced.

This National Park is a mecca for fishing enthusiasts. Forty-four lakes and innumerable streams hold masses of German brown, brook, rainbow, and cut-throat trout. The fish may not be particularly big, but there will be plenty. You need a Colorado license. Use of live bait is prohibited except under certain special conditions. Review special fishing regulations at park headquarters or at the nearest ranger station.

Since hunting is forbidden here, all forms of wildlife abound. Herds of elk and deer browse the high plains and slopes near the top of Trail Ridge Road during summer. Above treeline in the tundra area, you see the yellowbelly marmot, and the tiny Pika. Beaver are easy to observe.

If you are lucky you may be able to spot some bighorn sheep, the elusive symbol of Rocky Mountain National Park. The bighorns can see objects up to a kilometer or two away. And they are exceptionally sure-footed.

Below nine thousand feet or so you wander among forests of Englemann spruce, subalpine fir, and limber pine.

A favorite way to see this park and surrounding country is on horseback. Estes Park calls itself the "horse capital of Colorado" and horses can be leased by the hour or day; you can ride with a guide or on your own. Some stables offer breakfast rides, fishing trips, and other outings. Full details available at the Estes Park Visitors' Center.

Camping

In the Rocky Mountain National Park, Colorado's largest, campgrounds are first-come, first-serve, except for two where reservations may be made by mail or in person at the park or at the regional office,

655 Parfet St., Denver. No telephone reservations. Mail reservations are handled by Ticketron offices in San Francisco, or you may call the Park Service's Denver office, (303) 234-3095, for more details.

A few suggestions, among others: **Moraine Park Campground,** at 8,200 feet above sea level, one mile west of Moraine Park Visitor Center off Bear Lake Road; **Glacier Basin Campground,** elevation 8,500 feet, eight miles west of Estes Park on Bear Lake Road; **Longs Peak Campground,** elevation 9,500 feet, eleven miles south of Estes Park. Generally full during the summer season.

You can get complete listings of campsites in the park, with maps and regulations, at any ranger station.

One recommended campground in the Estes Park area: **Estes Park Campground,** five miles southwest of town on Colorado Highway 66. Wooded area ideal for tents and camping trailers.

More camping, fishing, and recreational facilities exist in the 782,000-acre Roosevelt National Forest, adjoining the park. Numerous small glaciers, remnants of ancient ice fields, and remote camping spots provide intimacy with the wilderness.

The Rocky Mountain National Park region is dotted with small towns that offer a blend of local history, outdoor recreation, and resort-style relaxation. Glen Haven is a pleasant little tourist hamlet that offers cabins for rent. Situated in a deep valley seven miles northwest of Estes Park, on the North Fork of the Big Thompson River. Stop in Glen Haven's small café and grocery store.

Granby and Grand Lake

It is sixty-two curvy miles from Estes Park to the town of Granby, elevation 8,369 feet above sea level, on the western side of the Divide. Allow yourself three hours for a leisurely drive, more if you can afford it. (Please note: this "Trail Ridge Road" is snowed in and closed during the winter.) Three sizable lakes—Grand Lake, Shadow Mountain and Granby Reservoir—make the Granby area a recreation center. Dude ranches abound. The Colorado River and its tributaries provide trout fishing. The lakes have been stocked with kokanee salmon, among other species, and they provide fair angling as well as a unique sport—snagging with treble hooks—during the early winter spawning season. Since the kokanee die anyway after they spawn, snagging is permitted to avoid wasting a food resource. Granby is also in the center of the Middle Park area, noted for its dude and cattle ranches, and lumbering.

The sleepy village of Grand Lake is a popular area for summer homes. The namesake lake, Colorado's largest natural body of water, and nearby Shadow Mountain Recreation Area have the nation's highest—two miles above sea level—chartered yacht club. Each summer, the group sponsors regattas and other boating events. In winter, the community of Grand Lake attracts snowmobilers.

Leave the Estes Park area east on US 34 through Big Thompson Canyon. The twenty-mile drive is among the most scenic mountain passages in the state, passing craggy rock cliffs as it parallels the Big Thompson River.

Loveland

Loveland, on the flat land east of the canyon's mouth, is named for the man who built a railroad through the canyon in 1877.

As you reach Loveland, stop at the **Rocky Mountain Pottery Factory.** It covers more than thirty thousand square feet and offers a vast collection of unique clay and ceramic objects. Also, be sure to visit the **Loveland Museum,** 503 Lincoln Avenue, for another look at the region's history. The museum features old photos, rugs, tools—even an ancient dental lab. **Boyd Lake Recreation Area,** east of town, has one hundred campsites and offers good fishing and boating on its 3,320 surface acres of water. Loveland is known for its **Cloverleaf Dog Track** (spring and summers only) and for its **Post Office;** the latter remails thousands of Valentine greetings with a special Loveland "Sweetheart City" postmark.

HOTELS AND MOTELS

Rates for double occupancy average as follows: *Deluxe* $55–$100, *Expensive* $35–$54, *Moderate* $21–$34, *Inexpensive* $14–$20.

ESTES PARK (Zip Code 80517)

Long's Peak Inn and Guest Ranch. *Deluxe.* So. St. Vrain Highway. Charming chalets and lodge accommodations for 80 to 90 guests. Horses. Restful, isolated. Riverside dining. Summer only. Well managed. Highly recommended.

Stanley Hotel. *Deluxe.* A stylish old summer resort hotel with Victorian rooms. Fine ambiance. Large outdoor pool. Tennis court. Children's playground. Three restaurants. Theater.

Hobby Horse Motor Lodge. *Expensive.* Open all year.

Lake Estes Motor Inn. *Expensive.* US Hwy. #34. Overlooks lake, with three heated pools, playground, horses available, pleasant rooms. Best Western establishment.

Holiday Inn. *Expensive to Moderate* in off season. At Hwys. # 36 and Colo. 7. Large establishment with large rooms, Olympic indoor pool, game area. Café and bar on premises. Favored by conventions.

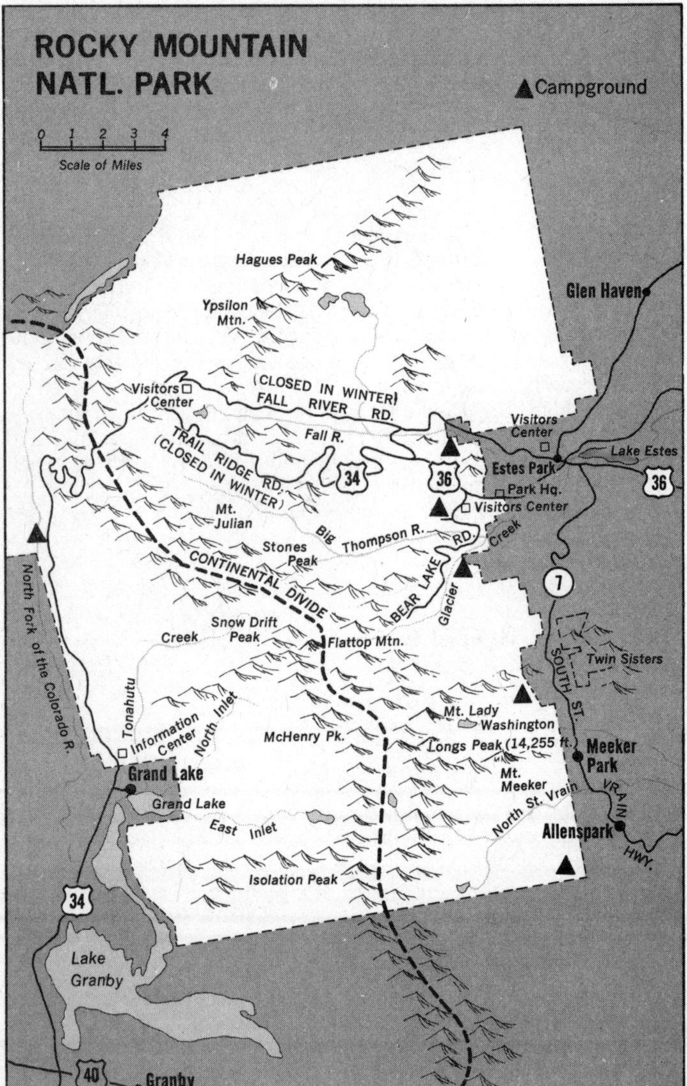
ROCKY MOUNTAIN
NATL. PARK
Campground
0 1 2 3 4
Scale of Miles
Hagues Peak
Ypsilon
Mtn.
Glen Haven
Visitors
Center
(CLOSED IN WINTER)
FALL RIVER RD.
Visitors
Center
Fall R.
TRAIL RIDGE RD.
(CLOSED IN WINTER)
34
36
Lake Estes
Estes Park
36
Park Hq.
Visitors Center
Mt.
Julian
Big Thompson R.
Stones
Peak
RD.
Creek
CONTINENTAL DIVIDE
BEAR LAKE
Glacier
7
North Fork of the Colorado R.
Snow Drift
Peak
Creek
Flattop Mtn.
SOUTH ST.
Twin Sisters
Tonahutu
Information
Center
North Inlet
Mt. Lady
Washington
McHenry Pk.
Longs Peak (14,255 ft.)
Meeker
Park
Grand Lake
Mt.
Meeker
VRAIN
Grand Lake
North St. Vrain
East Inlet
Allenspark
HWY.
Isolation Peak
34
Lake
Granby
40
Granby

Trail Ridge Motel. *Moderate.* 927 Moraine Ave. 1½ mi. southwest on State 66. Comfortable motel with pool, restaurant and cocktail lounge. Some efficiencies.

Miles Motel and Cottages. *Moderate to Inexpensive.* On Hwy. 7. Good location.

GRANBY (80446)

El Monte Lodge. *Expensive.* On US 40. TV, heated pool, playground, pets limited. Café and cocktail lounge.

Blue Spruce Motel. *Moderate.* Wood paneled rooms. Waterbeds. Always open.

Thunderbird Motel. *Inexpensive.* Small, comfortable motel accommodations. Commercial rates.

GRAND LAKE (80447)

Daven Haven Lodge. *Expensive.* ¼ mi. south on Main St. Small summer resort on the shores of Grand Lake. Boats, water-skiing, mini-golf, shuffleboard, badminton, heated pool. Cocktail lounge and two dining rooms.

Western Riviera Motel. *Expensive.* Well-run motel flanking lake. Open all year.

Riverside Guesthouses. *Moderate.* Large and small, well-furnished homes with fireplaces. Studios and accommodations for big families. Reservations needed. Recreation on premises. Quiet location, pleasant staff and management. Sauna. Long-time owners Ken and Martie Winters will give you their best. Recommended.

West Wind Cottages. *Moderate.* Summer accommodations.

LOVELAND (80537)

Best Western Coach House Motor Inn. *Moderate.* At I–25 and Hwy. #34. Large and new. Spacious units overlooking lake. Coffee shop. Cocktail lounge and disco-dancing.

Dreamland Motel. *Moderate.* 617 E. Eisenhower. Clean motel on main thoroughfare.

King's Court. *Moderate.* 928 Lincoln St. Small motel with heated pool, free coffee, nicely landscaped grounds. Café 3 blocks. Centrally located.

LONGMONT (80501)

Lamplighter. *Moderate.* 1642 N. Main St. Comfortable, large motel with indoor heated pool, TV, free coffee. Near supermarket.

Valeda Village. *Inexpensive.* 1417 Main. Small Friendship Inn. Color TV.

LYONS (80540)

Peaceful Valley Lodge and Guest Ranch. *Moderate.* Star Route. Chalets and main lodge. Indoor swimming. Horseback rides in summer. Cross-country skiing in Dec. and Jan. Under same ownership for many years.

RESTAURANTS

Price categories are approximate (for dinner, exclusive of drinks and tips): *Deluxe* $20 and up, *Expensive* $10–$20, *Moderate* $6–$9, *Inexpensive* below $6.

ESTES PARK

Nicky's. *Expensive to Moderate.* 1½ miles from downtown on US 34 West. Locally popular beef restaurant.

Old Plantation. *Moderate.* On Main St. Yankee pot roast, baked chicken, rainbow trout are specialties. Own pastries. Summer and fall only.

The Other Side Restaurant. *Moderate.* In National Park Village, Hwy. 34. Handsome restaurant overlooking lake. Great variety of foods. Coffee shop. Bar.

Rock Acres. *Moderate.* Bright and homey restaurant behind Stanley Hotel, overlooking mountains.

Timberline Steak House. *Moderate.* On Hwy. #7, 2 blocks from Holiday Inn. Good selection of dishes. Chicken liver, beef liver, trout recommended. Liquor. Open all year.

Coffee Bar Restaurant. *Inexpensive.* 162 E. Elkhorn Ave. Well-established café on main street. Good value. Long summer hours.

GRANBY

The Longbranch. *Inexpensive.* Home cooking on main street.

GRAND LAKE

Red Fox. *Expensive.* Continental restaurant. Dinner only.

Chuck Hole Cafe. *Inexpensive.* Home cooking.

LONGMONT

Old Prague Inn. *Expensive.* Genuine Czech food. Good wine list.

Sebanton French Restaurant. *Expensive to Moderate.* 424 Main. Small authentic French restaurant. Center of town.

The Armadillo. *Inexpensive.* Parkway shopping center. Mexican. Newish.

Furr's Cafeteria. *Inexpensive.* On Hwy. #287 north of Longmont. Good value.

LOVELAND

Summit. *Expensive.* 3208 W. Eisenhower. Handsome steak restaurant. Prime rib and King crab specialties.

Black Steer. *Moderate.* E. 5th & N. Lincoln. For meat eaters. Bar.

Bohemian Cottage Restaurant. *Inexpensive.* 8039 W. Hwy. 34. Quiet, cozy Czech establishment. Roast duck and dumplings, schnitzel recommended.

Rickshaw. *Inexpensive.* 14th and Boise. Loveland's Chinese entry. Good value.

COLORADO SPRINGS AREA

Scaling Pikes Peak

Colorado Springs is the state's second largest city, long famous as a watering place and summer resort. It was founded in 1871 by General William Jackson Palmer, promoter of the Denver and Rio Grande Railroad. General Palmer, who made or unmade towns depending on where he built his railroads, was also prominent in the planning of Colorado Springs, which he determined would have a gracious and cultured atmosphere not unlike his home town of London.

Pikes Peak looms over the city. In fact, the mountain seems to rise right at the end of Pikes Peak Avenue in downtown Colorado Springs. (There are many places in Colorado with the name "Springs"—Pagosa Springs, Poncha Springs, Steamboat Springs—but only Colorado Springs is referred to as "The Springs.")

Colorado Springs began as Colorado City in 1859, organized by a party of Kansas prospectors. The town advertised its free highway to the gold fields, mineral baths, and the Garden of the Gods (a spacious grove of sandstone monoliths).

The gold soon ran out and a decline in western travel during the Civil War set Colorado Springs on a period of decline. A flood washed away much of the settlement.

Then, in 1871, Palmer's railroad company purchased nearly ten thousand acres. From the beginning, Palmer promoted the region as a "scenic wonderland" and health resort. Pikes Peak was already a national landmark. Physicians extolled the dry air and bright sunshine, and several tuberculosis sanitariums were established. The town grew rapidly.

When new gold and silver finds—especially in Cripple Creek—brought these mountains to life again in the 1880s, Colorado Springs boomed, too. Within a few months of the first strikes, five mining exchanges had opened. Promoters and financiers rushed to Colorado Springs from across the nation. Bonanza kings invested part of their fortunes in substantial office structures and palatial houses. Between 1890 and 1900, the population increased from eleven thousand to more than twenty-three thousand; during the next decade Colorado Springs became one of the wealthiest cities per capita in the United States. The town never lacked patrons who contributed materially to its development.

Colorado Springs is still rated as one of America's most beautiful cities. For many tourists, Colorado Springs *is* the Rocky Mountains.

Local Attractions

The U.S. Air Force Academy, just north of town on I–25, welcomes tourists all year. The Visitors' Center provides details on exhibits, films, parades, and activities (all gratis). The roads through the 18,000-acre academy grounds are open during daylight hours. Just before noon, the cadets assemble outdoors and march in formation to the dining hall for lunch. This military parade is a worthwhile sight. At the end of May, you may see the academy's graduating ceremonies.

The academy's 17-spired chapel is as famous as it is architecturally controversial. Designed by Frank Lloyd Wright, it has been called "an accordion made of wigwams." But the chapel remains a classic example of Wright's ingenious designs. Protestant, Catholic and Jewish services can be held simultaneously and the three congregations may enter and leave without interfering with each other. Start with the academy's visitor's center; it is filled with historical photos, aviation models and data on cadet life. Self-guided tour.

The Garden of the Gods is world-renowned, too. More than two miles of paved roads meander among towering red sandstone cliffs, balanced rocks, and other dramatic formations. Once sacred ground to natives, the 1,025-acre park was donated to the city in 1918 by private owners. There are hiking trails. The trading post offers refreshments and telescopes.

And, of course, 14,110-foot-high Pikes Peak towers above it all. You have several options to reach the summit. You can motor in your own car; just follow US 24 west on Colorado Avenue. It takes about four hours to make the mountaintop that way. (A toll gate will exact a fee from you.)

For non-drivers, a Swiss cog railway climbs the summit in about three hours from a depot in Manitou Springs. Season is May through early October. (High tariff for adults, reasonable fares for children.) Each July 4, the Pikes Peak Auto Hillclimb attracts world-class race drivers who try to beat each other's time to the top. The winter snows usually close down part of the famous mountain highway.

Pikes Peak overlooks both the **Broadmoor Resort** and the Broadmoor community. Spencer Penrose built the hotel just after the turn of the century. This is a complete resort community in itself, with a luxury hotel, numerous dining rooms, conference center, several golf courses, outdoor pools, year-round ice-skating rink, a short ski slope in winter (with snowmaking machines), and a carriage museum. The staff, the dining facilities, and appointments are international. There are shops, stables, 16 tennis courts, and three eighteen-hole golf courses.

Above the Broadmoor Resort, visit the **Cheyenne Mountain Zoo.** See giraffes, bears, elk, deer, penguins, and other creatures. A little higher up to the south,the Broadmoor built its own small ski area. In summer, it attracts young enthusiasts to its Alpine Slide. Nearby **Seven Falls** cascade three hundred feet through a deep canyon. The entire area is beautifully lit at night and at Christmas; to find the Seven Falls, simply follow the South Cheyenne Canyon Road. And nature worshippers will want to see the **Cave of the Winds,** past Manitou Springs off US 24, atop scenic Serpentine Drive. Natural formations. Forty-minute guided tours four times each hour every day.

Farther up the Cheyenne Mountain Highway is the **Will Rogers Shrine.** Spencer Penrose built the one-hundred-foot granite tower in memory of his friend, the famed humorist. Photos, murals, and other reminders. A popular scenic overlook.

Cheyenne Mountain contains the bomb-proof headquarters of the North American Air Defense Command, known as NORAD. Here ninety computers and more than a million miles of communications lines watch the horizons for enemy missile attacks. Deep inside this hollowed-out mountain, fifteen buildings are supported on 1,319 steel springs weighing one thousand pounds each. Rock reservoirs hold six million gallons of water and steel blast doors protect the complex. (In case of a nuclear attack, these twenty-five thousand-pound gates can be closed in thirty seconds.) Positive identification is required, and no cameras or tape recorders permitted. Reservations are essential for all tours. For details, stop by the Visitors' Center south of US 24 on Peterson Boulevard.

Colorado Springs' Myriad Museums

The **Colorado Springs Fine Arts Center,** 30 West Dale Street, has a reputation for its contemporary art and for special exhibits of paintings and sculpture. The modern building has been praised by architects. Closed Monday.

The **Natural History Museum,** nine miles south of town on Nevada Avenue, offers zoology aplenty. More than seven thousand rare invertebrates from the jungles of the world. Adjoins the one thousand-acre Golden Eagle Safari Campgrounds and Resort, with hiking, boating, fishing. June through September.

The **National Carvers Museum** is at exit 158 from I–25. "The carving capital of America" sports over three thousand wood carvings collected from across the U.S. Also: carving classes and supplies. Open daily for guided tours, 9 A.M.–5 P.M.

The Pioneer's Museum beckons at 215 S. Tejon St. Local, Western, and Indian memorabilia. Daily except Monday. Free.

Prorodeo Hall of Champions and Museum of the American Cowboy at exit 147 of I–25 occupies a sleek new building. Large saddle collection, art gallery, live cattle and actual cowboy demonstrations, plus slide shows in two theaters. Open all year, except holidays, during business hours. Closed on Mondays. Admission fee.

Manitou Springs has the outdoor **Cliff Dwellings Museum.** Pueblos, tools, mummies, burial urns, and other remains of the Indian civilization that flourished here from A.D. 1100 to 1300. Seasonal.

The Hall of Presidents Wax Museum, on US 24 and south on 21st St., includes lifelike figures of each president and other notables: astronauts, the Court of Versailles, even Alice in Wonderland. Reminiscent of the famed Tussaud waxworks in Paris. Open at all seasons. A block away, at 21st St. and US 24, visit the **Van Briggle Pottery** building (actually an old railroad roundhouse). Here pots will be "thrown on the wheel" and you can see other phases of pottery-making. Free guided tours. Plenty of finished work to buy for souvenirs. Open daily except Sunday.

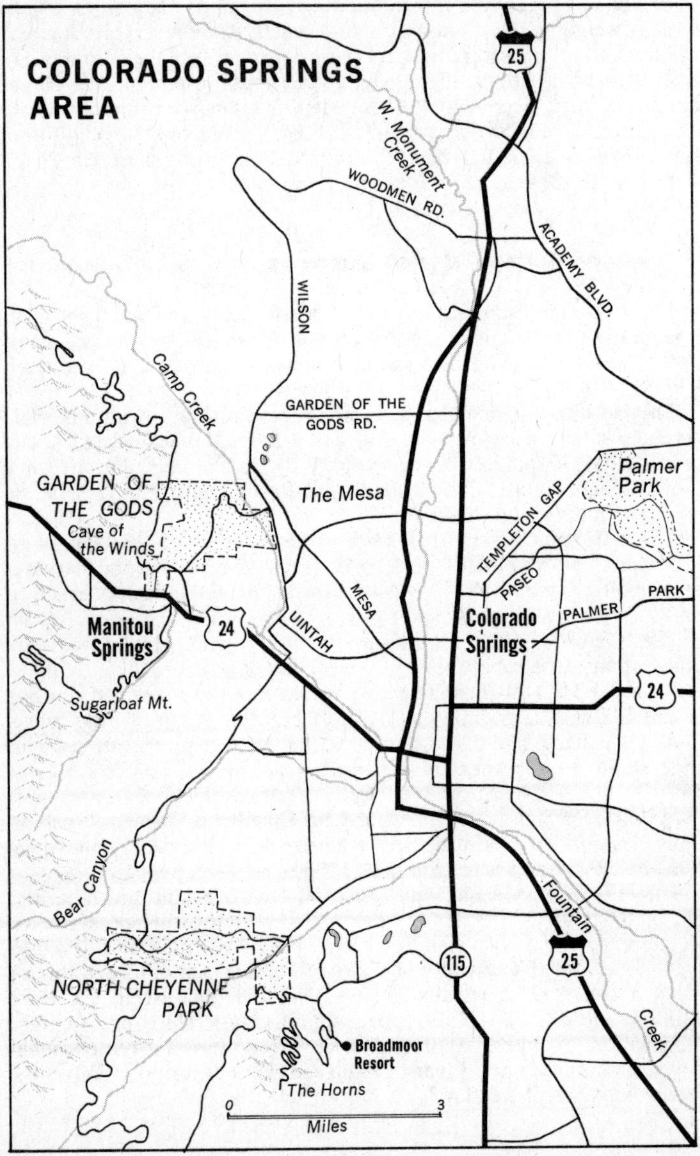
COLORADO SPRINGS AREA
25
W. Monument Creek
WOODMEN RD.
ACADEMY BLVD.
WILSON
Camp Creek
GARDEN OF THE GODS RD.
Palmer Park
The Mesa
GARDEN OF THE GODS
Cave of the Winds
TEMPLETON GAP
PASEO
MESA
PARK
PALMER
Manitou Springs
24
UINTAH
Colorado Springs
24
Sugarloaf Mt.
Bear Canyon
Fountain
25
115
NORTH CHEYENNE PARK
Creek
Broadmoor Resort
The Horns
0
3
Miles

One of the areas most popular family destinations: **Santa's Workshop** at the North Pole off US 24, on the foot of Pikes Peak. Kids can talk to Santa, his helpers, and other storybook characters. Tame reindeer, puppet and magic shows. Local artisans staff eight gift shops. Train and stagecoach rides. June through Christmas Eve; closed Thursdays. Touristy but fine for the young. Admission fee.

The **Western Museum of Mining and Industry,** at exit 156A across I–25 from the Air Force Academy, exhibits hardrock mining gear, ore samples, and assay demonstrations. Open all year, 9 A.M. to 4 P.M.

Flying W Ranch just west of Colorado Springs features an old western town. At suppertime you eat western chow and take in a wild-west show and musical. Reservations required. Open June to September.

South of Colorado Springs

If you drive forty miles south on I–25, you will reach Pueblo, at the confluence of the Arkansas and Fountain Rivers. Its main industry is the **CF&I Steel Corp.** (Tours available.) Pueblo is the trading center for the rich farm and ranch towns of the Arkansas Valley. Lakes, streams, campsites, and ranches of the **San Isabel National Forest** are all nearby. Pueblo is home of the **University of Southern Colorado, Pueblo Community College, Sangre de Cristo Arts and Conference Center, El Pueblo Museum** (operated by The State Historical Society), **Otterstein's Show Room** (vintage autos and Pueblo memorabilia), **Firemen's Museum,** and **Weisbrod Outdoor Museum** (World War II-era aircraft, at the airport east of the city). Five miles west is **Lake Pueblo** with good boating, fishing, and camping.

Royal Gorge

Fifty miles southwest of Colorado Springs on Highway 115 and US 50 there plunges the 1,200-foot-deep chasm named Royal Gorge. (Open year-round.) To reach the gorge, turn off the highway at US 50. Travelers plumb the rocky canyon depths via a steep incline funicular, or drive across a mighty suspension bridge—one of the world's highest. In addition, they can ride a thirty-five-passenger tram. Also, a miniature narrow-guage passenger train carries passengers along the chasm rim for a closer look. More adventurous types can make a raft trip down the Arkansas River as it splashes through the floor of the gorge. Details from Royal Gorge Rafting in nearby Canon City.

From Colorado Springs, on the road to Royal Gorge, is **Alta Vista Scenic Railway**—a four-mile ride through piñons and wildflowers. (Summer season.) US 24 continues gently uphill to Woodland Park, center of a dude ranch and recreation area. Seven miles farther is

Divide, where the road forks. State 67, turning left, offers a leisurely eighteen-mile drive through hay meadows and pine groves on the "back" side of Pikes Peak until, at the crest of Tenderfoot Hill, the once fabulously rich Cripple Creek-Victor gold fields stretch before you.

Cripple Creek and Victor

Cripple Creek and Victor, built on the side of a mountain, recently revived its mining industry thanks to rising gold prices. In the old days a half-billion dollars of the precious metal was dug from the surrounding hills. In those boom years—from 1890 to World War II—Cripple Creek was America's rough-and-tumble "promised land." Everyone came here: a young Jack Dempsey fought all comers for $50 a match; the late Groucho Marx, stranded between engagements, arrived in a grocery wagon. Journalist Lowell Thomas grew up in the neighboring town of Victor. By 1900, the town had forty stock brokers, sixty doctors, thirty-nine real estate brokers, and eight newspapers.

Today, Cripple Creek's few permanent residents depend mostly on tourists. Visitors come to ride **Cripple Creek and Victor Railroad,** a four-mile, forty-five-minute excursion in open cars through mining country. Guides provide a good narration. And there are photo stops at trestles and in mountain valleys. The **Cripple Creek District Museum** is housed in the once-busy railroad terminal. Exhibits re-create the city in which twenty-five thousand people once worked, brawled, got rich, or lost everything. The **Imperial Hotel** remains the local magnet for tourists. Built in 1896, the three-story brick inn was restored in the late 1940s. Not all rooms have baths, but the décor is authentic 1890s frontier elegance. The basement Gold Bar Room Theater offers a summer performance schedule of the Imperial Players. Their "melodrama" is accompanied by honky-tonk piano.

HOTELS AND MOTELS

Double-occupancy rates average as follows: *Deluxe* $55–$100, *Expensive* $35–$54, *Moderate* $21–$34, *Inexpensive* $14–$20.

COLORADO SPRINGS (Zip Code 80900)

The Antlers. *Deluxe.* Pikes Peak Ave. at Chase Stone Center. Located in the heart of downtown Colorado Springs. A modern, luxury, 15-story complex complete with lounge, coffee shop, and elegant dining room. Small rooftop heated pool. Bar, dancing, entertainment. Most rooms with good views of the

Peak. Barber and beauty shops, plus assorted fashionable stores. Hotel managed by Broadmoor Company.

Broadmoor Resort. *Deluxe.* 5 mi. south on US 85, 87, then west on State 122. This distinctive, world-famous resort is set on 5,000 acres. A center for large convention groups, facilities include large heated outdoor pool, saunas, many dining rooms, barber, beauty and other shops. Recreational facilities include elaborate golf, tennis, riding, skiing, ice rinks, boats, squash, handball, skeet, bicycles, scuba. Entertainment, dancing, movies. Large skating center.

Hilton Inn. *Expensive.* Modern hostelry. Near Garden of the Gods. Lovely view of Pikes Peak. Ideal for tourists. Especially spacious rooms and public areas. Good Western and Mexican dining. Meeting room facilities.

Holiday Inn-Central. *Expensive.* 8th and Cimarron Sts. Good location. Large motel with heated pool, restaurant, bar, dancing, entertainment.

Palmer House Motor Inn. *Expensive.* I–25 at Fillmore St. exit. Large, well-planned establishment with spacious rooms, heated pool, restaurant, cocktail lounge, dancing, entertainment.

Dravo Manor Motor Hotel. *Moderate.* 1703 S. Nevada. A small, well-kept motel with heated pool, restaurant, bar.

Imperial 400. *Moderate.* 714 N. Nevada. Modern, small chain motel with heated pool, basic necessities, cafe nearby. Good location for sightseeing.

TraveLodge-North. *Moderate.* 5700 N. Nevada. Large, modern motel with heated pool, playground; café not far. Free coffee.

Apache Court. *Inexpensive.* 3401 W. Pikes Peak Ave. 13 units.

Bel Air Motel. *Inexpensive.* 4000 N. Nevada Ave. Small but clean.

Belmont. *Inexpensive.* At Nevada and Arvada. Tiny pink motel on busy Colo. Hwy. #85.

Motel 6. *Inexpensive.* N. Chestnut at exit 64. Come early in day.

CANON CITY (81212)

Best Western Royal Gorge. *Expensive.* Heated pool, pets, restaurant, bar. Attractive rooms.

The Ramada Inn. *Expensive.* Newish motel on edge of Canon City, en route to Royal Gorge and mountains. Two swimming pools. Small convention area.

El Camino. *Inexpensive.* Attractive motel with mini-golf, playground, café ½ mi.

CASTLE ROCK (80104)

Motel 8. *Moderate.* 700 Park. Adjacent to Village Inn Pancake House.

CRIPPLE CREEK (80813)

Imperial Hotel. *Moderate* (except for summer season). Historic Victorian Cripple Creek Hotel. Imperial Dining Room.

Campgrounds

Garden of the Gods Campground, west on US 24 Business to 37th Street. May 30-September 15. Crowded. By reservation.

Pikes Peak Campgrounds, six miles west on I–25, exit 141, US Hwy. 24 to Manitou Avenue exit.

Diamond Campground, US Hwy. 24, then ½ mile north of Woodland Park on Colorado Hwy. 67; sites nestled in a pine forest.

RESTAURANTS

COLORADO SPRINGS

Broadmoor Hotel Dining Rooms. *Deluxe to Moderate.* In the Broadmoor Hotel. There are a number of fine restaurants in this complex: the *Broadmoor Tavern,* the *Main Dining Room,* the elegant *Charles Court,* the Edwardian *Penrose Dining Room* with a splendid view of Cheyenne Mountain, and the *Golden Bee,* an English pub of the 19th century that was brought over and rebuilt. The *Charles Court* has received several awards and boasts sophisticated gourmet menus and outstanding chefs. *Penrose Room* offers mountain views, Edwardian elegance and a Continental menu with four different veal dishes, fine filet mignon, fresh salmon, coq au vin. The longtime impresario here is Helmut Meyer, a Bavarian. Superb service.

London Grill. *Deluxe.* Distinguished English-style dining. Fine meats, superb appetizers including London grill, smoked salmon, wines. At Antlers Hotel.

Finn Dining and Drinking Establishment. *Expensive to Moderate.* 128 S. Tejon. Good western restaurant at old Alamo Hotel.

Village Inn. *Moderate.* 217 E. Pikes Peak Ave. in center of Colorado Springs. Located in an old church, this restaurant serves consistently good food, from a versatile menu. A Colorado Springs tradition. Cocktail lounge.

Black Angus. *Inexpensive.* 3330 N. Academy Blvd. Good value for meat eaters. Entertainment.

Flying W Ranch Chuckwagon. *Inexpensive.* 6100 Wilson Rd. A truly Western supper, served on tin plates by lantern light on picnic tables. Children's plates. Western entertainment follows dinner. This is a working cattle and horse ranch. Reservations required.

J. Muldoons. *Inexpensive.* 222 North Tejon. Mexican.

CANON CITY

Merlino's Belvedere. *Moderate.* 1330 Elm Ave. Locally popular Italian restaurant with bar.

Chile Wagon Restaurant. *Inexpensive.* 315 Royal Gorge Rd. Mexican food.

THE REST OF THE STATE

Summer in Roaring Fork Valley

In the Roaring Fork Valley of the central Rockies, Aspen offers as much to summer visitors as it does to winter skiers (see *Ski* chapter).

Aspen was transformed from a near-dead mining town into a year-round cultural and recreational center by Walter Paepcke, chairman of the Container Corporation of America. In 1945, Paepcke and a group of associates "discovered" the hamlet and decided it was the perfect setting for "a community of peace . . . with opportunities for man's complete life . . . ." The group brought over two thousand people to Aspen in 1949 for the Goethe Bicentennial Convocation to celebrate the German poet's "spirit of optimism." Participants included Albert Schweitzer, Thorton Wilder, and Thomas Mann. Concerts were held under a massive tent designed by famed architect Eero Saarinen.

The **Aspen Music Festival** continues as an annual event, now drawing visitors from all over the world. And the Aspen Music School is lively.

The Festival provides symphonic, chamber, contemporary, operatic, and choral works by a variety of performing groups. The programs usually run from late June through August. Some of the participants are students in the prestigious **Aspen Music School. Ballet West,** an international touring group, has open-air rehearsals in Snowmass Village and performances at Aspen High School. The **Aspen Writers' Conference** holds workshops and public performances in June and July, while the Aspen Leaves poetry group often sponsors discussions and open readings.

The summer **Aspen Institute for Humanistic Studies** regularly fetches renowned scholars for intensive discussions each June. Aspen's **International Design Conference** brings international architects, economists, graphic artists and designers together to discuss trends.

More traditional tourist fare is available, too. Aspen's Visitors' Center is in the Wheeler Opera House building on East Hyman Avenue. The **Historical Society Museum** at 6th and Bleeker provides tours of the town's silver-boom past.

Golf and tennis facilities are scattered throughout the area. Events range from rodeos and balloon races to an annual Ruggerfest rugby tournament. Within a twenty-five-mile radius of Aspen, outdoor types will find some twenty-five trout lakes and a thousand miles of trout streams, plus countless miles of hiking and riding trails. Mountains to challenge expert climbers are numerous, while backpackers find their Nirvana in the region. Not far from Aspen, up the Crystal River Valley, is Marble, where stone for the Lincoln Memorial and the Tomb of the Unknown Soldier was quarried.

West of Aspen on Colorado 82 along Maroon Creek, sightseers will discover the often-photographed Maroon Bells peaks. A glacial lake lies at the foot of the jagged, snow-topped mountain giants, the Bells. The area is part of the Maroon Bells/Snowmass Wilderness, with its many hiking trails.

Glenwood Springs

Colorado 82 continues from Aspen to Glenwood Springs, forty-two miles northwest. Glenwood, as residents call it, sits in the White River National Forest. The two million acres are renowned for all manner of open-air sports, even spelunking. The forest includes the Flat Tops Wilderness, a huge 117,800-acre plateau north of Glenwood Springs and Rifle, which extends into three counties. Allow a few hours for a

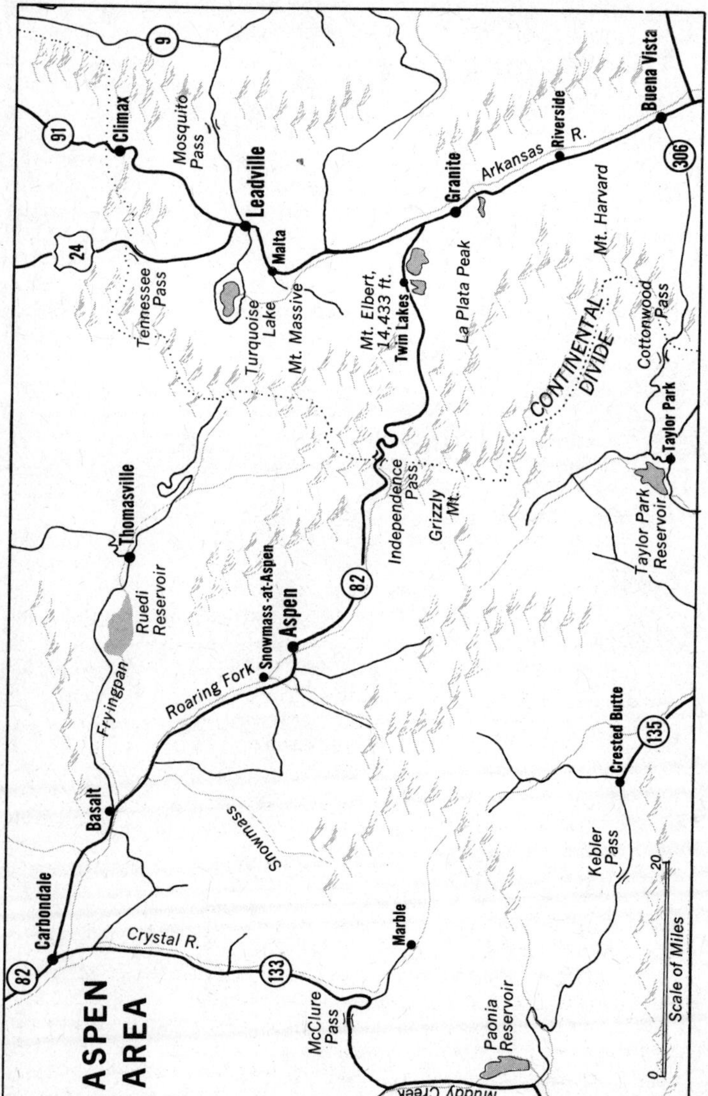
ASPEN AREA
Climax
Mosquito Pass
Leadville
Malta
Tennessee Pass
Turquoise Lake
Mt. Massive
Mt. Elbert, 14,433 ft.
Twin Lakes
La Plata Peak
Granite
Arkansas R.
Riverside
Buena Vista
Mt. Harvard
CONTINENTAL DIVIDE
Cottonwood Pass
Taylor Park
Taylor Park Reservoir
Independence Pass
Grizzly Mt.
Thomasville
Ruedi Reservoir
Fryingpan
Aspen
Snowmass-at-Aspen
Roaring Fork
Basalt
Snowmass
Carbondale
Crystal R.
Marble
McClure Pass
Paonia Reservoir
Muddy Creek
Kebler Pass
Crested Butte
Scale of Miles
0
20
9
91
24
82
133
135
306

hike to Hanging Lake and Spouting Rock, ten miles east of Glenwood Springs. The small lake was formed by erosion. Picnic sites.

Glenwood Springs' location at the confluence of the Roaring Fork, Crystal, and Colorado rivers make it one of the state's most popular river-rafting center. Local guides are available with trips of all lengths and difficulties.

Glenwood's original attraction, the acclaimed hot springs mineral baths, are always open to the public. In the 1880s, silver baron Walter Devereaux decided to convert the springs used by the Utes to a health resort for the rich. He built the two-block-long swimming pool, intended for use only by guests of the posh adjacent Hotel Colorado. By the early 1900s, so many wealthy and famous people came to the spa that a rail siding was installed beside the hotel to hold their private railroad cars. Teddy Roosevelt made the hotel his summer White House in 1901 while bear hunting in the nearby hills.

The mineral baths and vapor caves are open all year, with trained personnel on hand. Locals say the water is a quick cure for visitors' aching muscles and stiff joints after days in the nearby wild.

Each June, Glenwood Springs celebrates Strawberry Days as it has every year since 1889. Parades, a carnival, and free strawberries and ice cream courtesy of the local Kiwanis Club.

Leadville

The town of Leadville—87 miles east of Glenwood—remains a historical center. The community of 4,300 people owes its existence to a gold boom in the 1860s and 1870s. By 1880, Leadville counted thirty thousand citizens and became "the richest and roughest town in the world." English poet Oscar Wilde visited Leadville on his 1882 American tour. "I read the miners' passages from the *Autobiography of Benvenuto Cellini,*" Wilde recalled, "and they seemed much delighted. I was reproved by my hearers for not having brought him with me. I explained that he had been dead for some little time, which elicited the inquiry, 'Who shot him?' "

A department store chain and the Guggenheim fortune both began here.

Memories of those days are preserved in the **Heritage Museum and Gallery,** open summers only, at 9th and Harrison. The Healy House, built in 1878, is restored and serves as a museum to illustrate the bonanza mining period. On the same grounds is the Dexter Cabin, which looks like a log cabin from the outside but is finished inside with fine woodwork and hardwood floors. Daily, June to mid-October. Free.

The story of Leadville is largely the story of Horace Tabor. He came to the gold fields as a shopkeeper and put up a $17 grubstake for two miners in return for a one-third interest in whatever they found. The two men quickly stumbled onto the Matchless Mine, one of the richest silver veins ever uncovered. Tabor lavished his income from the mine—as much as $100,000 a month—on Leadville and Denver, building opera houses, grand homes, and other projects. He created Colorado's greatest scandal after he divorced his prim wife Augusta and married Elizabeth "Baby" Doe, a working-class woman thirty years his junior. Tabor was ruined when the value of silver plummeted in 1893. He died penniless in 1896. His last words to Baby Doe were "hang onto the Matchless." She did, in the vain hope it would again make millions. She died in Leadville during the cold winter of 1935.

The Leadville tragedy is remembered in the American opera, *The Ballad of Baby Doe,* which gave Beverly Sills one of her first roles with the New York Opera Company. (The opera is a staple in Central City.)

The **Matchless Cabin,** one mile out of town on East 7th Street, contains a small museum that tells the Tabor story to summer visitors. Tabor's original frame home at 116 East 5th Street has been preserved. Some of the rooms can be entered. A small gift shop sells relics, including copies of old newspapers. Tabor's Opera House on Harrison Avenue has also been restored. Daily tours, June through Labor Day.

Leadville remains a magnet for geologists, the area having produced more than $700 million in silver, lead, zinc. Molybdenum, a steel-hardening element used for military and industrial hardware, is also found nearby. Most of the free world's molybdenum comes from Climax, twelve miles north of Leadville.

The Leadville area boasts a nine-hole public golf course and many hiking trails. Several hundred lakes are close by, including Turquoise Lake, on the west edge of town, rimmed by bicycle trails.

For a closer look at the region's history, stop at Fairplay, an old mining camp east of Leadville on US 285. Here, the **South Park City Museum** re-creates the boom town of South Park City. Twenty-five original buildings were preserved and restored for public tours. A general store displays the necessities, and few luxuries, available to pioneers; a drug store is stocked with old nostrums and patent medicine bottles. The original **South Park Brewery,** now on the National Register of Historic Places, stands intact nearby. Mining and ore processing gear also on display. Open mid-May to mid-October.

Other mountain villages, such as Telluride to the south, hum with summer activity. The **Telluride Bluegrass and Country Music Festival** is held annually in June, and the **Chamber Music Festival** comes early in August. Just before Labor Day Telluride caps its summer season with an **International Film Festival** which sells out weeks in advance. The film program, kept secret until the Festival opens, is shown in the

Sheridan Opera House. Film stars appear here regularly, along with directors, writers and critics.

The Western Slope

Western Colorado is known as "Standing Up Country." Towering pine forests are dwarfed by the large peaks. In the southern part of the region, you may stop at the Uncompahgre National Forest with its full range of camping and recreational facilities. Just east, the mountain city of Montrose serves as a local vacation headquarters. Information on local ghost towns, campgrounds, jeep trips, and excursions into the rugged San Juan Mountains is available here. Also, the Ute Indian Museum in town commemorated Colorado's indigenous tribes. A monument to an Indian Chief and the grave of his wife, are on the grounds.

Montrose nestles near some outstanding recreation areas. Just to the north is the **Black Canyon** of the **Gunnison National Monument,** which is eighteen miles east of Montrose. Embracing 13,667 acres, this monument contains twelve miles of the deepest and most scenic portion of the gorge of the Gunnison River, one of the most amazing geological displays in the West. Here the river has cut into some of the earth's oldest base rocks to a maximum depth of 2,425 feet. Descent into the canyon is dangerous and difficult; visitors shouldn't attempt it without consulting a ranger first. The name Black Canyon comes from the smoky rock walls, as well as the sunless areas of the canyon.

On each rim, roads allow you to drive to panoramic points of observation. The South Rim is reached from US 50 on State Road 347. The North Rim is at the end of a fourteen-mile gravel road from State Road 92 east of Crawford. You will find camp and picnic grounds in these areas open from May through October.

The North Rim Road is usually closed by snows during the rest of the year, while the South Rim Road is open year-round. Campfire programs are conducted by rangers from mid-June to Labor Day. Otherwise, personnel are on duty all year at South Rim, and summers only on the North.

If you follow the Gunnison River for about thirty miles east of Montrose, you will reach the **Curecanti National Recreation Area,** comprised of three reservoirs—Blue Mesa, Morrow Point and Crystal. Blue Mesa Lake, twenty miles long, offers three campgrounds, boat ramps and water sports. A marina has rental boats and equipment for fishing and water skiing. Shore fishing for rainbow trout is best in early spring and late fall. The best salmon fishing usually starts in late June through August. Fishing is regulated by state laws. Be sure you have a current license.

Cimarron, 20 miles east of Montrose, has a narrow-gauge railroad exhibit with engine, coal tender, freight car, and caboose, displayed on an 1882 trestle.

The 469-foot-high Morrow Point Dam, farther along US 50, can be reached from Cimarron turnoff. Self-guided tours of the underground power plant daily from Memorial Day to Labor Day.

Boat tours are available on Morrow Point Lake.

Continuing north along the West Slope you will see Grand Mesa looming before you. Grand Mesa is one of the world's largest flat-top mountains with about 625 square miles of national forest. Deep canyons, waterfalls, abundant camp and picnic grounds, and more than two hundred lakes and reservoirs give outdoor enthusiasts yet another place to linger.

Grand Junction

The 18,000-acre **Colorado National Monument** lies at the southwest edge of Grand Junction, the West Slope's commercial center. Follow the Rim Rock Drive, two thousand feet above the Grand Valley below.

Five-hundred-foot-high Independence Rock, Window Rock, and Red Canyon may be seen from lookouts along the twenty-two-mile drive. Meadows of wildflowers and forests of juniper and pine surround the mountains. Wildlife protected by the National Park Service, roam the area. Dinosaur beds have been excavated here during the past decade. Stratified ramparts carved by time create a gallery of strangely beautiful natural sculptures.

The Visitors' Centers at park headquarters will assist the traveler in the area. Nightly programs by rangers during the summer. Campsites with excellent facilities and picnic areas are available. Well-marked trails beckon to hikers.

The town of Grand Junction got its name from the Colorado and Gunnison rivers meeting here. Summer events range from horse shows and rodeos to drag racing and balloon rallies. Local points of interest include the downtown **Museum of Western Colorado,** which presents the region's geological and social history.

Grand Junction possesses many tangible resources in a 250-mile radius. Uranium, lead, zinc, and other minerals have been mined here for years. Grand Junction is also becoming a national energy center. The Book Cliff Mountains and Piceance Basin to the north hold some of the nation's recoverable shale oil—perhaps some three billion barrels, or enough to power the entire nation for almost a century. It will be several years before a significant amount of oil is produced from the rock, but pilot plants already function. Paraho Development Company, a pioneer in oil shale research, offers public tours of its processing plant. Inquire locally.

For a brief but interesting side trip, make sure your gas tank is full before taking US 50 southeast out of Grand Junction. Nine miles up the highway is the tiny crossing called Whitewater. Turn right here onto State 141, and prepare to enter some of Colorado's wildest, loneliest canyon country, an area largely overlooked by most tourists. The highway, paved and well-maintained, stretches through sagebrush flats and dry washes for forty-four miles to Gateway, where it crosses the muddy, shallow Dolores River. For the next thirty-seven miles to Uravan, the road borders first the Dolores, and then the San Miguel (pronounced San M'gill) rivers, leading past towering red sandstone cliffs, polished by wind and sand into monolithic slabs, and often into the shapes of ships and pyramids.

Back in 1881, gold-seekers found a soft yellow-orange ore near what is now Uravan. Its main use was for coloring pottery. In 1898, several tons of this ore were shipped to France, and Mme. Marie Curie used it in experiments that resulted in the extraction of radium. For the next thirty years, this region produced about half the world's radium supply. A mill was built at Uravan to process vanadium, a steel-hardener, from the same ores. During World War II, in the crash program to develop a nuclear bomb, the waste rock in the tailings piles at the Uravan mill was reprocessed to extract the suddenly precious uranium which had been thrown away. The mill, now operated by Union Carbide, extracts uranium from local mines, and vanadium has become just a by-product.

Nineteen miles past Uravan, take the right fork to State 141 for the fifty-seven-mile drive to Dove Creek. This apparent wasteland has a strange, lonely beauty of its own, but you'll be glad to reach civilization once more at Dove Creek, center of a prosperous pinto bean-growing area. Total distance from Grand Junction to Dove is 169 miles. Dove Creek was little more than a raw frontier town until farmers from the dust bowl in eastern Colorado came in to conquer the arid flats. Zane Grey, the western author, lived here for some years.

Rifle

In the booming town of Rifle, sixty-two miles northeast of Grand Junction, you enter the heart of energy country. The population, now about six thousand, is projected to be 20,000 by 1985. Already, the nearby oil, gas, and shale fields have attracted many workers.

Growth has yet to affect Rifle's popularity as a big game hunting center; each autumn, hordes of transient elk and the nation's largest herd of mule deer cross the region on their way to winter pastures. Also in the fall: the **Garfield County Fair** on Labor Day attracts visitors and contestants from three states for parades and rodeos. The Colorado River near Rifle is noted for its trout fishing. At the entrance to Rifle Mountain Park, the state operates a large trout hatchery, to stock its streams and lakes each spring. Free tours.

Dinosaur National Monument occupies Colorado's northwest corner. This area of about 325 square miles in Colorado and Utah contains one of the world's largest concentrations of fossilized dinosaur bones. The remains of brontosaurs and other species of prehistoric creatures have been removed from the shales and sandstones of an eighty-acre tract within Dinosaur National Monument. Visitors may watch technicians as they expose and relief the bones of many kinds of dinosaurs and other prehistoric reptiles. There are now more than 2,000 fossilized bones on view as a permanent exhibit.

Among the exceptional features of the monument are deep, narrow gorges with sheer, strangely carved and delicately tinted sandstone cliffs. Lodore Canyon, cut by the meandering Green River, varies in depth from 1,000 to 3,300 feet.

A thirty-one-mile paved road from the Dinosaur, Colo., headquarters leads north into the heart of the canyon country. Scenic overlooks and the two-mile-long trail at Harpers Corner provide spectacular views of the Green and Yampa Rivers and their confluence at Steamboat Rock—over 2,500 feet below.

Southwest: The Durango Region

Durango is the hub of the state's southwest. Its countryside—memorable from a dozen John Wayne westerns—has made it a vacationers' mecca, surrounded by modern dude ranches. River rafting, horseback riding, jeeping all enjoy a great popularity.

A major local attraction: the **Durango and Silverton Railroad's** narrow-gauge train journey from Durango to the mining town of Silverton. The forty-five-mile trip takes you up the gorge of Rio de las Animas Perdidas (River of the Lost Souls), or simply the Animas River. Belching smoke and cinders, an ancient steam engine puffs through thick forests and along steep cliffsides for an unforgettable ride into yesterday. (Don't dress up for it, though. Coal dust! Also, you might want to arrange to take the slow-moving train just one way.)

The time in Silverton is just long enough for lunch and a stroll around the streets, to peer into abandoned buildings, and to browse among the curio shops. If you don't find any agates on the Animas River's gravel bars, numerous youngsters are anxious to sell you specimens of iron pyrite, azurite, malachite, or quartz crystal for fifty cents. Although it once boasted ten thousand residents, Silverton now has a

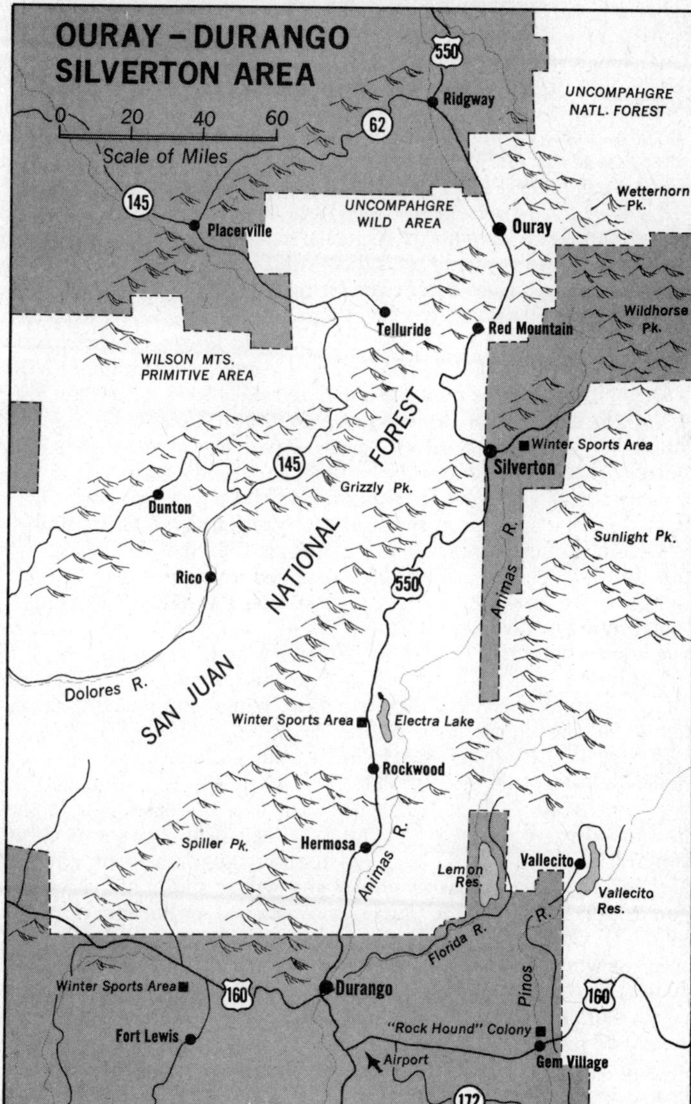
OURAY – DURANGO
SILVERTON AREA
0 20 40 60
Scale of Miles
550
Ridgway
62
UNCOMPAHGRE
NATL. FOREST
145
Placerville
UNCOMPAHGRE
WILD AREA
Ouray
Wetterhorn Pk.
Telluride
Red Mountain
Wildhorse Pk.
WILSON MTS.
PRIMITIVE AREA
FOREST
Winter Sports Area
Silverton
145
Grizzly Pk.
Dunton
NATIONAL
Animas R.
Sunlight Pk.
Rico
550
SAN JUAN
Dolores R.
Winter Sports Area
Electra Lake
Rockwood
Spiller Pk.
Hermosa
Animas R.
Lemon Res.
Vallecito
Vallecito Res.
Florida R.
Pinos R.
Winter Sports Area
160
Durango
160
Fort Lewis
"Rock Hound" Colony
Gem Village
Airport
172

thousand. It is the seat of San Juan County, which has the distinction of being so high and rugged that there isn't one acre of farmland in it.

To save time, some visitors prefer to ride up on the train and be met at Silverton by a member of the party who has driven the fifty miles via US 550, continuing north without returning to Durango. Trains run nearly all year, but the winter train only goes halfway to Silverton, is turned on a wye and returns to Durango. Reservations essential. Buy your tickets several days in advance, if possible.

Highway 550 rises from Silverton to 11,018-foot Red Mountain Pass (named for the reddish hue of the soil), strikingly beautiful in summer but impassable in winter. This is the "Million Dollar Highway," which follows a toll road route laid out by Otto Mears in the 1880s. The origin of the name is obscure. Some say it was so named because of the cost, while others contend it is because of the gold-bearing gravel.

Beyond the pass is Ouray (pronounced U-ray), a community nestled in a mountain pocket a mile and a half above sea level. This is the heart of the "Switzerland of the Rockies." Within a fifteen-mile radius of Ouray are seventy-one peaks, seven of which exceed the height of fourteen thousand feet. Nearby is the Camp Bird Mine. At one time it produced as much as four million dollars a year in gold. Ouray maintains a picnic area in Box Canyon where Canyon Creek plunges down a dark, misty gorge. If you can spare the time, take a Jeep trip into the high country along trails calculated to frighten even a mountain goat. The paved highways are as spectacular as the high trails to be navigated by Jeep.

While in Durango, inspect the **Strater Hotel,** which goes back to 1882. Guest rooms are furnished with genuine antiques to re-create the Victorian atmosphere. A "Gay Nineties" saloon and melodrama theater round out the summer experience.

If you drive Highway #550 north from Durango, you will see a modest sign on your right. It reads "Tamarron Resort". A guard at the gate screens all visitors. **Tamarron** is a five-star oasis that fetches discriminating vacationers from all over the world. The resort is surrounded by a National Forest, and the four hundred to six hundred guests can partake of both summer and winter sports of every kind. You can play tennis inside (during snowstorms), or outside (on lovely fall days). Golf fairways and platform tennis courts sit among conifer trees. In winter, Tamarron offers its own ski hill with its own short chairlift, cross-country instruction, sleigh rides and shuttle buses to nearby Purgatory, a bigger ski area. All year, children have their own supervised programs. Tamarron is worth a stop for its gourmet lunches and dinners as well. Deluxe accommodations in spacious condominiums or lodge rooms.

Mesa Verde National Park

Tamarron makes for an ideal overnight stop before you drive on and venture into Mesa Verde National Park. There is no other national park quite like Mesa Verde, which means "green table" in Spanish. The table is a plateau rising fifteen hundred feet above the surrounding valleys. In canyons hewn into the plateau, an early tribe of Indians grew corn with water brought in by primitive irrigation systems, and built apartment-like dwellings under overhanging cliffs. One settlement, called Cliff Palace, has two hundred rooms on eight levels. A study of tree rings indicates the area suffered a severe drought in the thirteenth century, and the Indians wandered away circa 1276. Thanks to the dry air and the protection of the caves, many well-preserved dwellings and artifacts were found by the first white men. The National Park Service has restored many of the ruins and conducts tours among them, with lectures about the people who lived in them seven hundred years ago.

After receiving an information packet from rangers at the park entrance, you follow the scenic road five miles to a campground/shopping complex where you can buy genuine native handicrafts. Park Point, ten miles from the entrance, offers a thirty-thousand-square-mile view over six mountain ranges in four states.

More cliff dwellings may be seen at the Hovenweep National Monument, northwest of Mesa Verde on the Colorado-Utah border.

Southern Outposts

On the way to Trinidad, south of Pueblo, watch for deer and antelope among the stretches of wild barley and porcupine grass.

In Trinidad, visit the restored 1869 adobe home of ranchero Felipe Baca and the Charles Addams-style mansion of pioneer merchant, cattleman, and banker, Frank Bloom. Of particular interest is the **Victorian Rose Garden** of the Bloom mansion. The **Trinidad Lake Recreation Area** is five miles west on Colorado 12.

Also south on I–25, you will enter Walsenburg, a town originally named La Plaza de Los Leones (Square of the Lions) by Spanish landowners. In 1870, the citizenry adopted its present name in honor of Fred Walsen, community leader and the owner of the area's general store.

Continue west from Walsenburg via US 160. Turn south onto Colorado 12 and drive to La Veta, a small community. Stop at the Fort Franciso Museum. Colorado 12 gradually climbs amid stands of scrub oak and pinion pine to San Isabel National Forest with its picnic grounds, campgrounds, and hiking trails. Just outside of town, to the left, you will see the Devil's Stairstep, a unique geological phenomenon of huge rock walls which radiate like spokes of a wheel from the peak's summit.

Returning to La Veta, drive approximately thirty-six miles west on US 160 to **Fort Garland State Museum** (small entrance fee). The fort was built in 1859 and commanded by Kit Carson in 1866/7. The fort is now a National Historic Landmark maintained by the Colorado Historical Society.

Drive ten miles west of Fort Garland on US 160 and turn north on Colorado 150 to the **Great Sand Dunes National Monument.** Located at the western base of the Sangre de Cristo mountains in the San Luis valley, the Great Sand Dunes offer visitors a vista of sands piled to seven hundred-foot summits. These sand dunes cover some 575 square miles. There is a campground nearby.

Del Norte, west of the Great Sand Dunes National Monument, lies in a niche of the Rio Grande National Forest on the banks of the Rio Grande River. Its geography has made it a headquarters for rafting, backpacking, hunting, and many other outdoor sports. Ghost towns dot the surrounding hills. From Del Norte, it is easy to reach the Wheeler Geological Area, a jagged limestone formation that juts up out of the spruced-lined valley.

Northeast

The broad, flat plains of northeast Colorado hold more than the lush fields and expansive cattle ranches which you see there today. This was where the prairie schooners and prospectors first reached the Colorado Territory along the South Platte River. They came on three trails—the North Smoky, Middle Smoky, and South Smoky—depending on their points of origin. Together, the routes were called the Starvation Trail.

The land is dotted with reminders of those early days: a now-dry buffalo wallow, wagon ruts along the old trails or at the site of stagecoach stops. Gnarled cottonwoods overhang cutbank pools where yellowheaded blackbirds forage among cattails. Red mallow, prairie gentian, sand lily, arrowhead, and other flowers unknown in the rest of the country grow in wild profusion. The area still contains a few flint arrowheads and petrified wood. In the cliffs of Pawnee Buttes, fossilized remains of prehistoric camels and horses have been found.

The small farm towns of eastern Colorado—Brush, Yuma, Sterling—all hold mementos of the past. The village of Julesburg in Colorado's northeast corner was, for a time, a major rest stop on the California Trail and a station of the Overland Stagecoach line. Here Sam Clemens (Mark Twain) rested on his way to Nevada. (He describes his Colorado experience in *Roughing It.*) Here journalist Ned Buntline came to find a young Buffalo Bill and make him famous. A local historical museum, just off I–80, illustrates those days.

South of Julesburg on US 385, you come to the **Bonny Reservoir State Recreation Area.** Camp, swim, fish, go boating, relax in this Colorado plains oasis. Just north of the Reservoir is Beecher Island, site of a bloody Indian battle. A stone marker there tells the story.

Three small cities anchor the region. Fort Morgan, sixty miles northeast of Denver, is a hub of regional commerce and agriculture. The town grew from a cavalry stockade built in 1874 to protect incoming travelers from marauding Indians. Fort Morgan is now the center of a lush farming area rich in corn, sugar beets, cattle, and dry beans. A pleasant place for a day's quiet rest.

Greeley, which began as a temperance colony sponsored by editor Horace Greeley, is about fifty miles northeast of Denver. Memberships in the original colony sold for $15 to "men of strict temperance and good character." Sobriety made for a sober attitude which paid results: all around the town, you notice fields of sugar beets, barley, and other crops. Some of Colorado's excellent corn-fed beef comes from this region. As a young college professor in Greeley during the 1930s, author James Michener conceived his novel *Centennial.* Some critics believe Michener modeled his fictional town after the nearly-deserted village of Keota, forty miles northeast of Greeley.

In the same vicinity, Fort Collins may well be the most sophisticated community in Northern Colorado. With 61,300 inhabitants, it is the largest. There are twenty thousand Colorado State University students here. Fort Collins also has several book stores, numerous foreign car dealers and shops catering to the young. Among the sightseeing attractions: the **CSU Agricultural Campus** at Laurel Street (research facilities) and **Lincoln Center** at 4th and Magnolia (theater, concerts, and art galleries).

Southeast

Looping south past the old wagon train stop of Cheyenne Wells, approach the town of Chivington. From this campsite in 1864, Colonel John Chivington marched a rag-tag band of volunteers along the road that leads over a sagebrush wasteland to the cottonwood groves along Sand Creek. In a surprise attack on Arapaho and Cheyenne tribes camped there, the colonel and his men massacred them all.

A bit farther south lies a fertile strip of land among the Arkansas River. Wagon trains often camped here. Twenty miles east in Lamar (pop. 7,800) a monument called **"The Madonna of the Trail"** honors the women who settled the West.

Proceed east to Las Animas, past dense fields of wheat and sorghum. You find yourself in one of Colorado's most intensely cultivated areas. At Las Animas, the **Kit Carson Museum** houses mementos of the famed mountain man. It was near Las Animas that Zebulon Pike first sighted the peak that bears his name. Be sure to visit **Bent's Old Fort,** a National Historic Site. The old trading post built on this site in the 1850s has been restored. Builders used sketches made by early travelers in the days when Bent's Fort was the department store of the frontier: Indians and trappers would come here to exchange furs and pelts for supplies, tools, cloth, and other goods. The fort also became a Grand Central Station for travelers from both ends of the Santa Fe Trail. The restoration of Bent's Fort is considered to resemble the original settlement in almost every detail. Now there are also shops, refreshments, tourist information.

Follow the Arkansas River to Rocky Ford, "the melon capital of the world." Each August, Melon Day is celebrated yearly with sixty tons of free watermelons. Rocky Ford is also known for the production of seeds. When you buy a packet of zinnia seeds, for instance, chances are one in three that they were raised in Rocky Ford. This fertile region also produces cantaloupe, cucumber, pumpkin and squash seeds, and onions.

HOTELS AND MOTELS

Accommodations in the *non*-ski resort areas of Colorado tend to be friendly and warm toward the motoring family. These operations depend heavily on summer revenue and hostelry to make travelers comfortable.

The price categories in this section, for double occupancy, will average as follows: *Deluxe* $45–$100, *Expensive* $30–$44, *Moderate* $20–$28, and *Inexpensive* $15–$19. For a more complete description of these categories, see the *Hotels and Motels* section of *Facts at Your Fingertips* at the front of this volume.

ALAMOSA (Zip Code 81101)

Alamosa Lamplighter Motel. *Moderate.* Main Street. Enclosed pool. Restaurant and bar.

Best Western Alamosa Inn. *Moderate.* On US 160 at 285. Heated pool, saunas, dining room and cocktail lounge. A Best Western motel.

Walsh Hotel. *Inexpensive.* 617 6th St. Some bathless rooms.

ALLENSPARK (80510)

Allenspark Lodge. *Inexpensive.* Small, woodsy inn.

BRUSH (80723)

Best Western Thunderbird Motor Inn. *Moderate.* 44 units. Year-round.

Empire Motel. *Inexpensive.* 1408 Edison. Small motel with heated pool, large shaded lawns. Miniature golf next door.

BUENA VISTA (81211)

Sumac Lodge. *Moderate.* On State 24. Pond, mountain view, shaded lawn, coin laundry.

Topaz Lodge. *Moderate.* On State 24. Small, friendly.

BURLINGTON (80807)

Best Western Chaparrel Motor Inn. *Moderate.* ½ mi. north on State 385. Heated pool, playground, pets limited.

Western Motor Inn. *Moderate.* Off US 24. Pets, restaurant, and coffee shop.

CORTEZ (81321)

Ramada. *Expensive.* 79-room motel. Playground. Low season: Oct. to May.

Sands. *Expensive.* 1000 E. Main St. Heated indoor pool, playground, pets, restaurant and lounge. Small conventions.

Turquoise Motor Inn. *Moderate.* 535 E. Main St. Heated pool, restaurant and cocktail lounge. Free airport bus.

CRAIG (81625)

Holiday Inn. *Expensive.* New.

Best Western Inn. *Moderate.* 36 rooms.

DEL NORTE (81132)

Rio Grande Motel. *Inexpensive.* Clean.

DURANGO (81301)

Tamarron Resort. *Deluxe.* 18 mi. north of Durango. Magnificent lodgings in one of the nation's more outstanding resorts. Hotel rooms and large condo accommodations for 1,600 persons. Many sports facilities, including own golf course, own ski lift, sleigh rides, XC instruction, tennis clinics, children's programs. High-class dining. One of the best self-contained resorts in the state. Outstanding location, good security.

Quality Inn Summit. *Expensive.* On County Rd. 203.

Holiday Inn-Durango. *Expensive to Moderate.* On US 160 & 550. Four blocks from famous railroad depot. Recommended.

Best Western Durango Inn. *Moderate.* West of town on Hwy. # 160. Recommended.

General Palmer House. *Moderate.* 567 Main Ave. A Victorian relic, restored. Small pets, café, bar. D & RGW narrow-gauge railroad depot adjacent.

Strater Hotel. *Moderate.* 669 Main Ave. Well-restored hotel. Guest rooms with antiques. All public rooms are in authentic Victorian décor. Special honeymoon suite. Delightful cocktail lounge, good dining room. Diamond Belle Bar, melodramas in the Diamond Circle Theater during summer.

Silver Spruce. *Inexpensive.* 2929 N. Main Ave. Pets, café 2 blks. Small, comfortable motel.

FORT COLLINS (80521)

Holiday Inn. *Expensive.* I–25 and Hwy. 14. Chain member with heated pool, restaurant, cocktail lounge, entertainment, beauty shop, mini-golf.

Lamplighter. *Expensive.* 1809 N. College. A Best Western establishment.

Ramada. *Expensive.* 3709 E. Mulberry. Indoor pool. Coffee shop. Lower prices in winter.

Best Western University Motor Inn. *Moderate.* 914 S. College Ave. Opposite Colorado State University, with heated pool, café.

Motel 6. *Inexpensive.* 3900 E. Mulberry. Basic facilities. Check in early during day; often filled up by 3 P.M.

GLENWOOD SPRINGS (81601)

Antlers Best Western Motel. *Expensive.* 80-unit motel. Clean.

Ramada Inn. *Expensive.* I–70 exit 116. Reliable lodging. All facilities. Meeting and convention area.

Holiday Inn. *Expensive to Moderate.* 2 mi. west at I–70 exit. Chain member, with heated pool, saunas. Restaurant, bar, entertainment, dancing. Car needed.

Glenwood Hot Springs Lodge. *Moderate.* Center on I–70. Large, well-maintained motel with comfortable rooms. 2-block-long hot-spring pool, terrace dining, playground, sports-wear shop, cocktail lounge. Recommended. Good value.

Hotel Denver. *Moderate.* 7th and Cooper Sts. Popular with businessmen. Pets, restaurant, cocktail lounge.

GRAND JUNCTION (81501)

Holiday Inn. *Expensive.* 755 Horizon Dr. Massive convention motel. Two cafés, free airport shuttle.

Howard Johnson's Motor Lodge. *Expensive.* 752 Horizon Dr. Café. Cocktail lounge.

Ramada Inn. *Expensive.* On I–70. Well-known chain hostelry.

Best Western Bar-X Motel. *Expensive to Moderate.* 1600 North Ave., ½ mi. northeast on US 6, 24. Modern, with spacious grounds; across street from golf course. Heated pool, restaurant, bar, free airport bus.

American Family Lodge. *Moderate to Inexpensive.* 721 Horizon Dr., 3½ mi. north at I–70 airport exit. Attractive rooms, heated pool, playground, pets. Café opposite.

Holiday Motel. *Moderate to Inexpensive.* 1460 North Ave., on US 6. Limited pets, free coffee. Café adjacent.

GREELEY (80631)

Holiday Inn. *Expensive to Moderate.* At 8th Ave & 6th St.; Centrally located high-rise. 100 rooms with TV. Sauna. Recommended for frequent travelers. Nightly entertainment.

Ramada. *Expensive to Moderate.* U.S. Hwy. 85 (Evans). Outdoor pool. Pleasant dining room with fireplace.

Apple Valley Inn. *Moderate.* 84th Ave. and 16th St. Near college.

Greeley Lamplighter. *Moderate.* Hwys. 85 and 34. A Friendship Inn.

Inn Towne Motel. *Moderate.* 1803 9th St. Comfortable motel. Free coffee, some kitchen units available. Café 3 blocks.

TraveLodge 6. *Inexpensive.* 721 13th St. Basic accommodations.

GUNNISON (81230)

Colorado West Motel. *Moderate.* 3 blocks east of Main. King and queen beds. Indoor pool and Jacuzzi. Good location. Recommended.

Tomichi Village Inn. *Moderate.* Pleasant motel near Western State college. Heated pool. Dining room.

LAMAR (81052)

Cow Palace Inn. *Expensive.* 1301 N. Main. Locally important motor hotel with attractive tropical courtyard and dining facilities. Shopping mall.

Lamar TraveLodge. *Moderate.* 1201 N. Main. For small conventions.

El Mar Motel. *Inexpensive.* 1210 S. Main St. Small, modern, heated pool, cocktail lounge and restaurant.

LEADVILLE (80461)

Best Western Silver King Motor Inn. *Expensive to Moderate.* Large, modern hotel with sauna, restaurant and cocktail lounge. Pets OK.

MESA VERDE NATIONAL PARK (81330)

Far View Motel. *Expensive.* At Navajo Hill, 15 mi. from park entrance. Private balconies provide a view of the canyon. Camping sites available. Cafeteria. Summer reservations advisable.

MONTROSE (81401)

Red Arrow Motel. *Expensive.* 1 mi. east on US 550. Attractive rooms in this motel with heated pool, playground, free coffee, sun deck. Café nearby.

Black Canyon Motel. *Moderate.* 1 mi. east on US 50. Small, with well-furnished rooms, heated pool, playground, restaurant next door. Free airport bus.

Lazy I G Motel. *Moderate.* 1 mi. east on US 50. Very small, has deluxe rooms, heated pool, free coffee, playground.

OURAY (81427)

Twin Peaks. *Expensive.* Clean, sleek Best Western establishment. Nicely landscaped. Closed in winter.

Box Canyon Motel. *Moderate.* At the mouth of the canyon, with a spectacular view. Playground, pets, free coffee. Horses available. Cafe nearby.

Ouray Chalet. *Inexpensive.* On US 550, State 789. Small motel with sundeck, free coffee. Café nearby.

PAGOSA SPRINGS (81147)

Best Western Pagosa Lodge. *Deluxe to Expensive.* Resort-type accommodations on edge of town. Tastefully decorated throughout. Tennis, swimming, golf. Coffee shop.

Pagosa Spring Inn. *Moderate.* 2 blks. south of US 160. Very small inn with mineral-water baths, delightful rooms, cocktail lounge and restaurant, pets.

PUEBLO (81001)

Pueblo West Resort. *Expensive.* 251 McCulloch Blvd. Very attractive motel with heated pool, restaurant and cocktail lounge. 18-hole golf course, tennis courts, heliport.

Ramada Inn. *Expensive.* I–25 and U.S. 50 East. Motor hotel with heated pool, good dining room, cocktail lounge, playground, beauty shop, free airport bus.

Super Eight Motel. *Expensive to Moderate.* Highway 50 West. A three-story, 80-room newcomer.

Best Western Town House. *Moderate.* 8th St. at Santa Fe Ave. Medium size with heated pool, dining room, coffee shop, cocktail lounge.

Holiday Inn. *Moderate.* 4001 N. Elizabeth. Swimming pool, sauna, dining room, cocktail lounge.

Rambler Motel. *Moderate.* 4400 N. Elizabeth St. Heated pool, 24-hour café nearby.

Regal 8 Inn. *Moderate to Inexpensive.* 960 Hwy. 50 W. Chain motel.

RIFLE (81650)

Midland Hotel. *Moderate.* Good value.

Shaler Motel. *Moderate.* Singles available.

SALIDA (81201)

Western Holiday Motor Hotel. *Expensive.* Clean accommodations.

SILVERTON (81433)

Grand Imperial Hotel. *Expensive.* 1219 Greene. Victorian hotel with saloon. Open all year.

STERLING (80751)

Best Western Coach House. *Expensive.* A 72-room facility off I–76 and Highway 6.

Holiday Inn-Sterling. *Expensive to Moderate.* At jct. I–76. All the expected amenities.

Sterling Motor Lodge. *Moderate.* 731 N. 3rd St. Playground, pets limited, free coffee. 24-hour café nearby.

TRINIDAD (81082)

Country Club Motor Inn. *Deluxe.* Nice rooms with oversize beds, heated pool, playground, beauty and barber shops, restaurant with good salad bar. Best Western chain.

Holiday Inn. *Expensive.* Quiet location.

Frontier Motel. *Moderate.* 815 Goddard Ave. 25 units with tile baths. TV.

WALSENBURG (81089)

Rambler. *Moderate.* I–25 and 160. Playground. Café.

RESTAURANTS

Dining out in Colorado towns can be great fun for the traveling family. Many of the smaller towns have different or unusual restaurants featuring local specialties, such as Mexican food. Prices are for the medium-price items on the menu. For other worthwhile restaurants, check the hotel listings. Restaurants are in order of price category.

Restaurant categories are as follows per person: *Deluxe:* $19 and up, *Expensive:* $10–$18, *Moderate:* $6–$9, and *Inexpensive:* under $5. These prices are for appetizer or soup, entrée, and dessert. Not included are drinks, tax or tips.

ALLENSPARK

Fawn Brook Inn. *Expensive to Moderate.* Austrian menu. Tables outside in summer. Rustic and pleasant. Owner is chef.

DURANGO

Canyon Restaurant-Tamarron. *Deluxe.* 18 miles from Durango. International cuisine in the grand manner. Supper a la carte. Appetizers include smoked trout. Excellent wild game. Long wine list. Tuxedoed waiters. Obligatory 15% service charge. Lovely view of National Forest.

Assay Office. *Expensive.* 3206 N. Main. Well-run. Locally popular. Lounge.

Palace. *Expensive.* 119 Main St. Victorian Restaurant. Fresh trout and 20 other entrées. Central. Cocktail lounge.

San Juan Dining Room. *Expensive.* At Tamarron. Well-lighted dining room with good view. Bright glassware and décor. Chandeliers. Attentive service.

Bar D Chuckwagon Suppers. *Inexpensive.* Cowboy-style dinner in outdoor setting. 7 days a week, summers only. Entertainment. Good for large families. Reservations needed.

FORT COLLINS

Nico's Catacombs. *Expensive.* 115 S. College. A downtown gourmet restaurant. Long menu.

Red Garter. *Moderate.* 117 Linden St. Fish restaurant. Entertainment. Beer garden in summer. Bar.

Tico's Foods of Mexico. *Moderate to Inexpensive.* 333 West Drake. Well-known local Mexican restaurant. Cocktails.

Washington Bar and Grill. *Inexpensive.* American theme restaurant with trolley cars, flags, stained glass decor. Popular with students. Beer and wine at reasonable prices.

FORT LUPTON

Branding Iron. *Moderate.* Western-style highway café.

GLENWOOD SPRINGS

Buffalo Valley Inn. *Moderate.* 3½ mi. southeast on State 82. In a rustic, Western setting. Steaks and ribs prepared over an old-time applewood cooking pit. Small bar. Good value.

Fireside Inn. *Moderate.* Bright family restaurant. Sizzlers. Salad bar.

Los Desperados. *Inexpensive.* West Glenwood Springs. Mexican cooking. Margaritas.

GRAND JUNCTION

Cork & Embers. *Expensive.* Candlelit steak restaurant. Nice salad bar. Cocktails.

Bonanza Sirloin Pit. *Moderate.* Locally popular. Steaks.

Dusty's Chile. *Inexpensive.* 710 North Ave. Local family café.

Furr's Cafeteria. *Inexpensive.* Excellent value.

GREELEY

The Gondolier. *Moderate.* 9th St. and 18th Ave. Good Italian food.

Red Steer. *Moderate.* 3 miles north of town. Banquet facilities.

Eat'N Place. *Inexpensive.* Excellent value. Has smaller portions for light eaters, seniors, children.

Garden Kitchen. *Inexpensive.* Chinese dinners. Own rolls and pastries.

La Cocina. *Inexpensive.* 2410 8th Ave. Mexican.

KITTHEDGE

The Prospect. *Expensive.* Shrimp, lobster, crab legs for year-round clientele.

LOUISVILLE

Blue Parrot. *Inexpensive.* Spaghetti and beef.

Colacci's. *Inexpensive.* 810 Main St. This restaurant makes its own pasta and spicy foods. Cocktail lounge. Frequented by people from Boulder and Denver.

MONTROSE

Glenn Eyrie. *Expensive.* Well regarded for its gourmet dining.

OURAY

1876 Restaurant. *Expensive.* An interesting menu that changes daily, plus steaks. Beams and paneling from a 100-year-old mine and period lamps make up the charming décor. Cocktails. Closed in winter.

Coachlight. *Expensive to Moderate.* Dine in Victorian atmosphere.

Casa de Cafe. *Moderate.* Mexican food. Summer only.

PAGOSA SPRINGS

Eagle & the Owl. *Expensive.* For gourmets.

PUEBLO

Fireside Restaurant. *Expensive.* 801 Highway 50. Old, established restaurant.

Top o' the Town. *Expensive.* 4201 Elizabeth St. Specialties are prime rib, steak, seafood.

Ignacio's Restaurant. *Moderate.* 4205 N. Elizabeth. Mexican food.

Three Thieves. *Moderate.* 720 Goodnight Ave. A quiet restaurant near park.

Golden Dragon. *Inexpensive.* Exit 101 at I–25. Good value.

Royal Fork. *Inexpensive.* 2160 Hwy. 50 W. Buffet.

RIFLE

Midland Lounge & Restaurant. *Moderate.* Serves three home-cooked meals a day.

Audrey Bakery. *Inexpensive.* Home cooking three times a day.

SALIDA

The Spa. *Moderate.* A restful, quiet dining room with a view of the surrounding mountains. Focus is on steak and trout with children's plates. Own baking. Open 6 A.M. to 10 P.M., winter to 8 P.M.

Salida Inn. *Moderate to Inexpensive.* Locally popular. Good beef. Liquor.

SILVERTON

Grand Imperial. *Moderate.* Pleasant hotel dining room with varied menu. Salad bar, own baking. Cocktail lounge.

The French Bakery Restaurant. *Inexpensive.* Simple dishes, well-cooked. Open all year.

Silver Wolf Cafe. *Inexpensive.* Home cooking. Open all year.

TELLURIDE

Powder House. *Expensive.* Known for its good seafood.

Sofio's. *Moderate.* Mexican food. Popular with local people.

INDEX

LANGUAGE/30

For the Business or Vacationing International Traveler

In 24 languages! A basic language course on 2 cassettes and a phrase book . . . Only $14.95 ea. + shipping

Nothing flatters people more than to hear visitors try to speak their language and LANGUAGE/30, used by thousands of satisfied travelers, gets you speaking the basics quickly and easily. Each LANGUAGE/30 course offers:

- approximately 1½ hours of guided practice in greetings, asking questions and general conversation
- special section on social customs and etiquette

Order yours today. Languages available:

ARABIC	GREEK	JAPANESE	RUSSIAN
CHINESE	HEBREW	KOREAN	SERBO-CROATIAN
DANISH	HINDI	NORWEGIAN	SPANISH
DUTCH	INDONESIAN	PERSIAN	SWAHILI
FRENCH	ITALIAN	PORTUGUESE	SWEDISH
GERMAN	TURKISH	VIETNAMESE	TAGALOG

To order send $14.95 per course + shipping $2.00 1st course, $1 ea. add. course. In Canada $3 1st course, $2.00 ea. add. course. NY and CA residents add state sales tax. Outside USA and Canada $14.95 (U.S.) + air mail shipping: $8 for 1st course, $5 ea. add. course. MasterCard, VISA and Am. Express card users give brand, account number (all digits), expiration date and signature.
SEND TO: FODOR'S, Dept. LC 760, 2 Park Ave., NY 10016-5677, USA.

INDEX

(The letters H and R indicate Hotel and Restaurant listings)